Summer Bridge
Grades 3

Editor: Julie Kirsch

Layout Design: Tiara Reynolds

Inside Illustrations: Magen Mitchell

Cover Design: Chasity Rice

Cover Illustration: Wayne Miller

ISBN 978-1-60022-446-1

Table of Contents

The *Summer Bridge Reading* series is designed to help children improve their reading skills during the summer months and between grades. *Summer Bridge Reading* includes several extra components to help make your child's study of reading easier and more inviting.

For example, an **Assessment** test has been included to help you determine your child's reading knowledge and what skills need improvement. Use this test, as well as the **Assessment Analysis**, as a diagnostic tool for those areas in which your child may need extra practice.

Furthermore, the **Incentive Contract** will motivate your child to complete the work in *Summer Bridge Reading*. Together, you and your child choose the reward for completing specific sections of the book. Check off the pages that your child has completed, and he or she will have a record of his or her accomplishment.

Examples are included for each new skill that your child will learn. The examples are located in blue boxes at the top of the pages. On each page, the directions refer to the example your child needs to complete a specific type of activity.

Summer Reading List

Babbitt, Natalie
Tuck Everlasting; The Eyes of the Amaryllis

Ballard, Robert D.
Finding the Titanic

Banks, Lynne Reid
The Indian in the Cupboard

Barrett, Judi
Cloudy with a Chance of Meatballs

Berenstain, Stan and Jan
Berenstain Bears Accept No Substitutes Big Chapter Books™

Blume, Judy
Tales of a Fourth Grade Nothing

Brink, Carol Ryrie
Caddie Woodlawn

Bruchac, Joseph
Skeleton Man

Collier, James Lincoln and Christopher Collier
The Bloody Country

Coville, Bruce
My Teacher Is an Alien

Creech, Sharon
Walk Two Moons

Curtis, Christopher Paul
Bud, Not Buddy

Dahl, Roald
James and the Giant Peach; Charlie and the Chocolate Factory

DiCamillo, Kate
Because of Winn-Dixie

Erickson, John R.
The Original Adventures of Hank the Cowdog

Fitzhugh, Louise
Harriet the Spy

Gardiner, John Reynolds
Stone Fox

Gutelle, Andrew
Baseball's Best: Five True Stories

Hamilton, Virginia
The House of Dies Drear

Haskins, Lori
Spooky America: Four Real Ghost Stories

Henry, Marguerite
King of the Wind: The Story of the Godolphin Arabian

Howe, Deborah
Bunnicula: A Rabbit-Tale of Mystery

L'Engle, Madeleine
A Wrinkle in Time

Levine, Gail Carson
Ella Enchanted

Lobel, Arnold
Grasshopper on the Road; Book of Pigericks: Pig Limericks

MacLachlan, Patricia
Sarah, Plain and Tall

McMullan, Kate
Dinosaur Hunters

O'Dell, Scott
Sing Down the Moon

Rockwell, Thomas
How to Eat Fried Worms

Sachar, Louis
Sideways Stories from Wayside School

Scieszka, Jon
Knights of the Kitchen Table

Silverstein, Shel
Where the Sidewalk Ends

Sobol, Donald J.
Encyclopedia Brown series

Steig, William
The Amazing Bone; Amos & Boris; Sylvester and the Magic Pebble

Steptoe, John
Mufaro's Beautiful Daughters: An African Tale

Stoutenburg, Adrien
American Tall Tales

White, E. B.
Stuart Little; Charlotte's Web

Williams, Margery
The Velveteen Rabbit

Summer Bridge Reading RB-904094

Incentive Contract

List your agreed-upon incentive for each section below. Place an *X* after each completed exercise.

	Activity Title	X	My Incentive Is:
9	It Means the Same		
10	Opposite Meanings		
11	It Sounds the Same		
12	Change the Beginning		
13	Change the Ending		
14	What Does It Mean?		
15	More Than One Meaning		
16	Figuring Out the Meaning		
17	Nonsense Words		
18	Like or As		
19	Comparing Two Things		
20	It's a Figure of Speech		
21	What's the Similarity?		
22	Do They Agree?		
23	Almost Late		
24	Flower Pressing		
25	Emma's Job		

	Activity Title	X	My Incentive Is:
27	Mapping It Out		
28	Air Pressure		
29	Antonio's Lizards		
31	Field Trip		
33	The Five Ws		
34	Primates		
35	What's in a Name?		
36	Kenyon's Finch		
37	Insects		
38	Aesop's Fables		
39	Mike and Moe		
40	Traffic Rules		
41	The Saguaro Cactus		
43	Compost Pile		
45	Planet Earth		
46	The Titanic		

	Activity Title	X	My Incentive Is:
48	Whales	X	
50	Why Did That Happen?		
51	Sara's Day		
52	Beavers		
53	The Neighborhood Fort		
55	That's a Fact		
56	Is That a Fact?		
57	What Makes You Think That?		
58	Kick Ball		
59	Chris's Adventure		
61	A Camping Trip		
63	The Junior Detectives		
65	The Shortcut		
67	Firefighters		
69	What Do You Think?		
70	What's the Problem?		
71	The Grass Is Always Greener		

	Activity Title	X	My Incentive Is:
72	A Day at the Lake		
74	Helen Keller		
75	Rattlesnakes		
76	Taking Care of Teeth		
78	Wolves		
80	Which Book Have You Read?		
81	Chewing Gum		
83	Paul Bunyan		
85	Alphabetical Order		
86	What Do You Want to Know?		
87	Book Directories		
88	A Specialized Dictionary		
89	Guide Words		
90	So Much Information		
91	Illinois		
92	Plan It Out		

Assessment Test

Read the passage and answer questions 1–9.

Choosing a Pet

Choosing the right pet is not simple. You cannot just fly by the seat of your pants, because the decision that you make will have lasting consequences for you, your family, and the pet you choose. Before choosing a pet, you must consider many things.

First, decide whether you are ready for the daily responsibility of caring for another life. It will be up to you to make sure that your pet is well cared for, even if you are tired, sick, or have other things to do. Also, consider the amount of free time that you will have each day to spend with your pet. Dogs need to be walked and played with every day. A lizard does not require as much care— especially the walking part!

If you think that you are ready to take care of a pet, consider how you want to spend time with it. Do you think that it would be fun to have a playful pet, like a dog, or would you be happier with a pet that is quieter, such as a hamster, fish, or bird?

Next, think about the size of pet that could live comfortably in your home. Do you have a yard? Some animals need room to run outside, while other pets can live quite happily in the house.

Finally, visit your local animal shelter before heading to the pet store. You will find a variety of animals there that need loving homes. Your next pet might be at a shelter waiting to share your home, your love, and your life!

1. Underline the sentence that tells the main idea.

2. List three supporting details.

_____

_____

_____

3. Write a synonym of *simple*. _____

4. Write an antonym of *sick*. _____

5. Write a homophone of *need*. _____

6. Write a simile about a happy pet._____

_____

© Rainbow Bridge Publishing   Summer Bridge Reading RB-904094

7. Circle the idiom located in the first paragraph.

8. Complete the analogy. Kitten is to cat as _____ is to dog.

9. Why do you think the author wrote the passage "Choosing a Pet"?

    A. to entertain readers with interesting stories about pets

    B. to inform readers about the things they should consider when choosing a pet

    C. to persuade readers to adopt homeless pets

10. Using the Venn Diagram below, compare and contrast two types of pets.

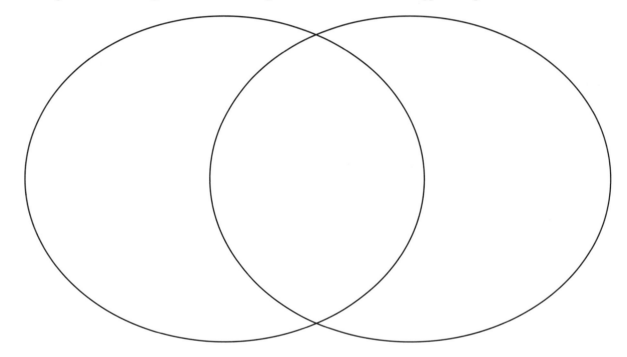

11. Read the following sentences. Write *O* if the sentence is an opinion. Write *F* if it is a fact.

_____ Cats are better pets than dogs.

_____ Pets need responsible care.

_____ Everyone should have a pet.

_____ All animals make good pets.

12. On another sheet of paper, write a story from a puppy's point of view about the child who is adopting it.

Assessment Test

Read the passage and answer questions 13–17.

Marcy's Bike

Marcy rode her new bike to Danielle's house. Danielle and Marcy took turns riding the new bike. They each rode it around the block several times. Marcy showed Danielle how she could ride her bike without holding on to the handlebars. Danielle wanted to try, too. Danielle started riding and shouted, "Look, no hands!" Then, Danielle fell on the sidewalk. She stood up right away. Marcy asked if she was all right. Danielle said, "I'm fine, but I think your handlebars are twisted."

13. Which of the following events happens second?

    A. Danielle falls on the sidewalk.

    B. Marcy rides her new bike to Danielle's house.

    C. The girls take turns riding Marcy's new bike.

14. Who are the main characters in the story? _____

Where does the story take place? _____

What is the problem in the story? _____

_____

15. How do the handlebars become bent? _____

16. What do you think will happen next? _____

_____

17. Read the following sentences. Write *C* beside the sentence that states the cause. Write *E* beside the sentence that states the effect.

_____ The handlebars on Marcy's new bike become bent.

_____ Danielle loses her balance and falls off Marcy's bike.

© Rainbow Bridge Publishing

Assessment Analysis

Check Assessment Test answers using the answer key provided. Match the questions with incorrect answers to the sections below. To provide extra practice in problem areas, refer to the pages listed under each section.

1. Choosing the right pet is not simple.
2. Decide whether you are ready for the daily responsibility of caring for a pet. Consider how much time you want to spend with your pet. What size of pet could live comfortably in your home?
3. easy
4. well
5. knead, kneed
6. Answers will vary.
7. fly by the seat of your pants
8. puppy
9. B;
10. Answers will vary.
11. O, F, O, O
12. Stories will vary.
13. C;
14. Marcy and Danielle, Danielle's neighborhood, Danielle falls off Marcy's new bike and bends the handlebars.
15. Danielle falls off the bike.
16. Answers will vary.
17. E, C

Number(s)	Skill	Page Number(s)
1	Main Idea	34–38
2	Reading for Details	39–43
3–4	Synonyms and Antonyms	9–10
5	Homophones	11
6	Similes and Metaphors	17, 19
7	Idioms	20
8	Analogies	21–22
9	Author's Purpose	76–77
10	Compare and Contrast	45–48
11	Fact or Opinion	55–56
12	Point of View	81–82
13	Sequencing	23–27
14	Character Analysis	71–74
15	Drawing Conclusions	61–67
16	Predicting Outcomes	57–59
17	Cause and Effect	50–53

It Means the Same

A **synonym** is a word that has the same or nearly the same meaning as another word. A synonym may be used in place of another word while not changing the meaning of the sentence.

Examples: The man carried all of his money in a brown *sack*. The man carried all of his money in a brown *bag*. The man carried all of his money in a brown *pouch*.

Choose a synonym from the box for each italicized word. Write the word on the line following its italicized synonym.

required	plans	constructed	pupils	finished
trip	place	country	sprinkling	welcomed

1. The fourth-grade students were going on a two-day *journey* _____ to learn more about their state's history.

2. Everyone was excited about the trip and knew that good *arrangements* _____ must be made in order to have a successful adventure.

3. When planning, they considered the weather, *necessary* _____ clothing, and how much money they would need.

4. The day that the trip began, it was *drizzling* _____ in the morning.

5. But, that did not bother the *students* _____, because each had brought a raincoat.

6. The bus traveled through one *rural* _____ town after another until it reached the State History Museum.

7. Once inside, they were *greeted* _____ by Ms. Handler, a guide, who took them through the museum.

8. The students learned that the state's capitol had been *built* _____ many years ago.

9. After the guide *completed* _____ the tour, the students thanked her and left to continue their trip.

10. Before heading to the next *stop* _____, the students ate the lunches that they had prepared before leaving home that morning.

Opposite Meanings

An **antonym** is a word that has the opposite meaning of another word.
Example: The *little* dog played with its new toy. The *big* dog played with its new toy.

Unscramble each of the following words. The underlined letter is the first letter of each unscrambled word. Select a word from the box that is the antonym for the unscrambled word. Then, write it on the line next to the unscrambled word.

| prompt | increase | find | calm | treasure |
| exaggerate | refuse | enormous | question | tense |

	Scrambled Word	**Unscrambled Word**	**Antonym**
1.	ypol<u>d</u>wan	_____	_____
2.	l<u>a</u>low	_____	_____
3.	so<u>l</u>e	_____	_____
4.	tmo<u>s</u>ry	_____	_____
5.	snerw<u>a</u>	_____	_____
6.	<u>t</u>nyi	_____	_____
7.	r<u>t</u>yda	_____	_____
8.	axe<u>r</u>lde	_____	_____
9.	hs<u>t</u>ar	_____	_____
10.	eu<u>r</u>edc	_____	_____

Extra! On another sheet of paper, write the words to your favorite song. Then, replace several of the words with their antonyms. How does this change the song?

It Sounds the Same

Homophones are words that are pronounced the same but are spelled differently and have different meanings.

Example: Mom went *to* the meeting at school. Dad went, *too*. The *two* of them met my teacher.

Complete the following sentences by circling the correct homophone. Then, on a separate sheet of paper, write a sentence using the other homophone.

1. The (bough, bow) of the tree hung low over the sidewalk.

2. Liz had been sick for four days and was (board, bored) with staying in bed.

3. The wranglers watched the (heard, herd) on the range.

4. Ben and Alex went (threw, through) the passage that led into the cave.

5. An (ark, arc) is a type of boat.

6. In (witch, which) shop did you find your new shoes?

7. Dad stopped and asked for the (way, weigh) to the stadium.

8. The camper put a (great, grate) over the fire and boiled water on it.

Change the Beginning

A **prefix** is a group of letters that is added to the beginning of a word. A prefix changes the word's meaning.

Example: pre + mature = premature

In the box below is a list of prefixes and their meanings. Study the prefixes and use them to complete the chart at the bottom of the page. Write each word's prefix and its base word. Then, use the information in the box to determine the word's meaning. The first one has been done for you.

pre = before	in = within
re = again	dis = not
bi = two	non = not or reverse of
un = not; opposite of	mis = wrong

	Word	Prefix	Base Word	Meaning
1.	bilingual	bi	lingual	speaking two languages fluently
2.	predetermine			
3.	redraw			
4.	misinterpret			
5.	nonviolent			
6.	disagree			
7.	intake			
8.	prepay			
9.	untie			
10.	rename			

Change the Ending

A **suffix** is a group of letters that is added to the end of a word. A suffix changes the word's meaning. Suffixes may also change a word's part of speech. For example, a verb may become a noun, a noun may become an adjective, or an adjective may become an adverb.

Examples:

write + er	verb to noun	Jane writes every day.
		Jane is a writer.
star + less	noun to adjective	That star is bright tonight.
		It is a starless, cloudy night.
happy + ly	adjective to adverb	John is a happy boy.
		John skipped happily on his way.

Notice that to change *happy* to *happily* the *y* changed to an *i* before the suffix *ly* was added. Also, when a word ends with a silent *e*, keep the *e* before adding a suffix that begins with a consonant. Drop the *e* before adding a suffix that begins with a vowel.

Complete the chart using the following suffixes. Use each suffix only once.

ist = person who does	ment = concrete result of
less = without	ful = full of
able = capable of	ward = in the direction of
al = related to; like	ship = state; condition

Base Word	Part of Speech	Base Word + Suffix	Part of Speech
1. entertain	_____	_____	_____
2. peace	_____	_____	_____
3. out	_____	_____	_____
4. thought	_____	_____	_____
5. art	_____	_____	_____
6. excite	_____	_____	_____
7. relation	_____	_____	_____
8. music	_____	_____	_____

What Does It Mean?

Some words have more than one meaning. You can tell which meaning is being used from the context of the sentence.

Example: The ticket taker *admitted* Alan into the theater after the movie started.
(Here, *admitted* means *permitted* or *allowed*.)
Nancy *admitted* that she had not done her homework.
(Here, *admitted* means *confessed* or *acknowledged*.)

Circle the letter next to the correct definition of each italicized word.

1. Jane was wearing an *olive* shirt with a tan skirt and socks.

   A. an evergreen tree

   B. a fruit

   C. a color

2. I saw the horse *bolt* from the barn during the heavy rainstorm.

   A. a rod to fasten a door

   B. a roll of cloth

   C. dart off; dash

3. Chris went to hear the *band* play at the city's annual spring festival.

   A. a strip of material

   B. a group of musicians

   C. to join together

4. We smelled an *odd* odor when we entered the basement.

   A. left over after pairings; remainder

   B. strange or peculiar

   C. not even

5. The police arrested the driver at the scene of the accident and *booked* him for reckless driving.

   A. entered charges against

   B. made reservations

   C. printed pages that are bound together in a volume

6. After the long hike, Mike saw a blister forming on his *sole*.

   A. the only one

   B. a flatfish

   C. the bottom of the foot

7. We walked several blocks before we were able to *hail* a taxi.

   A. icy precipitation

   B. signal

   C. greet with enthusiasm

8. The *light* in the corner of the room flickered just before it burned out.

   A. not heavy

   B. lamp

   C. bright

14

More Than One Meaning

Each word listed has more than one meaning. At the bottom of the page are definitions of the words. After each word, write the letters corresponding to its definitions.

Example: Word: skip _____x, y_____

Mini-dictionary: x. to follow directions out of order

y. to move lightly from one foot to the other

Words:

1. palm _____
2. fiddle _____
3. court _____
4. vessel _____
5. mask _____
6. harp _____
7. prompt _____
8. sore _____
9. glare _____
10. cabinet _____

Definitions:

A. a meeting room in a king's residence

B. a stringed instrument that is played with a bow

C. to dwell on a subject for a lengthy amount of time

D. a tube in the body in which fluid travels

E. the flat part of the hand between the fingers and the wrist

F. a face used for disguise

G. a shine with a harsh, brilliant light

H. to move hands and fingers restlessly

I. tender, painful

J. a cupboard with doors and shelves

K. ready; on time

L. an enclosed area where some ball games are played

M. to assist an actor by saying his next words

N. a type of tree

O. a stringed instrument that is played by plucking with the fingers

P. a large boat

Q. to stare angrily

R. a place where judges hear cases

S. a body of advisors of a head of state

T. a container for holding something

U. angry

V. to cover up; hide

W. a spot on the body

Figuring Out the Meaning

At times, you may not recognize a word in a sentence, but there are ways to figure out what the word means. One way is by determining its part of speech. Decide what part of speech the word is first, what function it has in the sentence, and then, what it actually means. Another way to figure out what it means is to look at the other words in the sentence and to think about what they mean. These other words are hints that are called **context clues**.

Use context clues to choose the word that completes the sentence. Circle the word.

1. _____ is one of Tom's favorite subjects.

   Astronaut   Astronomy   Atmosphere

2. He _____ likes to follow the movement of the stars.

   especially   establish   exceptionally

3. Tom was delighted when his family gave him a _____ for his birthday.

   telegram   telephoned   telescope

4. Part of his birthday present was a camping trip with his father in a park where _____ were good for stargazing.

   constellations   conditions   conjunctions

5. When Tom went to the park, he took the necessary equipment with which to make his _____.

   observes   orbits   observations

6. Tom saw several _____ including Orion and the Big Dipper.

   consultants   constellations   confirmations

7. He had a great time and asked if his father would take him on another _____ to observe the stars.

   explore   expedition   experience

Nonsense Words

There is a nonsense word in each pair of sentences below. Read each sentence.
Then, write a word on the line that makes sense in place of the nonsense word in
both sentences.

1. Isabel and Brett rode their bikes to the *flibber* down the street.

We watched Gretchen *flibber* the car in the driveway.

The nonsense word *flibber* means _____.

2. The little, white dog is Tyrone's new *prackle*.

Would you like to *prackle* this cat?

The nonsense word *prackle* means _____.

3. My mom asked me to *tirth* the baby to sleep.

When we were on the beach, I found a beautiful *tirth* with a fossil leaf imprint.

The nonsense word *tirth* means _____.

4. Do not step on the *blape* in the sidewalk!

While making breakfast, I can *blape* the eggs on the pan.

The nonsense word *blape* means _____.

5. I cannot chew gum, because it will *verg* to my braces.

My dad asked me to pick up every *verg* in the yard.

The nonsense word *verg* means _____.

6. I can tell time on my new *jeffa*.

Will you *jeffa* me at my swim meet?

The nonsense word *jeffa* means _____.

Like or As

A **simile** is a comparison of two unrelated things. Similes often use the words *like* or *as* to compare the two unrelated things.

Example: Rachel runs *like* a deer. She is as tall *as* a skyscraper.

Select a word from the box to complete each of the following similes.

1. The theater was as black as _____ before the movie started.

2. Jared was a quiet as a _____ as he studied for the test.

3. My dad's new shoes are as _____ as a new penny.

4. The airless ball is as _____ as a pancake.

5. Taylor's sister _____ like a monkey on the jungle gym.

> mouse
> swings
> shiny
> midnight
> flat

Use the similes in the box to complete the following sentences.

flew like a rocket	excited as bees in a bonnet
mad as a wet hen	looked like a stuffed pig
howled like a banshee	loud as 100 marching bands

6. When my friends and I bought tickets for the ball game, I was so ecstatic that I

_____.

7. All of us were as _____

to be going to the big game.

8. The first batter's baseball _____ out of the ballpark.

9. I ate so much popcorn that I must have _____.

10. One player was as _____ when the umpire called him out.

11. The roar of the crowd sounded as _____.

Comparing Two Things

> A **metaphor** is a comparison of two unlike things. It does not use the comparison words that are found in similes.
>
> **Example:** The moon was a lamp lighting up the night.

Circle the two words being compared in each sentence. Then, write how the two words are alike or what it is about them that is being compared.

1. The row of trees are soldiers standing at attention.

_____

2. From the airplane, the cars below were ants crawling along the highway.

_____

3. The circus clowns were sardines packed in one car.

_____

4. The sound of waves lapping the shore reminded me of dogs slopping water.

_____

5. The fans' stamping feet in the bleachers were drums beating inside my head.

_____

Summer Bridge Reading RB-904094

It's a Figure of Speech

An **idiom** is a figure of speech. Often, it is a phrase. It says one thing and means another.

Circle the letter next to the correct meaning of the italicized idiom in each sentence.

1. He is *a big cheese* at the high school.
   A. a cafeteria worker   **B.** the principal   **C.** a very important person

2. When I met the doctor, she gave me a *dead fish* handshake.
   A. limp   **B.** strong   **C.** wet

3. Tommy would *give you the shirt off his back* if necessary.
   A. lend you his shirt   **B.** help you any way he could   **C.** keep you warm

4. She did not talk about her family, because she did not want to reveal *the skeletons in her closet.*
   A. her family secrets   **B.** where she kept the trash   **C.** the end of a scary story

5. My mom is *the top dog* at the office.
   A. the loudest one   **B.** the one in charge; the boss   **C.** the office supplier

6. Let us *bury the hatchet* and get on with our lives.
   A. forget the past   **B.** stop chopping trees   **C.** go to the movies

7. The kid who always hides my books is a real *thorn in my side.*
   A. prickly plant   **B.** bothersome person   **C.** ticklish person

8. I really *put my foot in my mouth* when I offered to bake all of the cakes for the bake sale.
   A. spoke before thinking   **B.** hurt my mouth   **C.** was angry

9. The kid with the whiny voice is not *my cup of tea.*
   A. making the right tea   **B.** my kind of person   **C.** friendly to me

10. *The sky is the limit* when it comes to how many cookies you sell.
    A. the boxes are blue   **B.** cookies are delicious   **C.** the number is limitless

What's the Similarity?

analogies

An **analogy** is a comparison or relationship between two or more things that may otherwise not be alike. To complete an analogy, first determine what the relationship between the words is. Then, determine what word could be added to keep the relationship the same.

Write the word from the box that completes each analogy.

1. Subtraction is to _____ as division is to multiplication.

2. Anchor is to ship as brake is to _____.

3. Humidity is to _____ as arid is to desert.

4. _____ is to tracks as bus is to road.

5. _____ is to river as dolphin is to ocean.

6. Deep is to _____ as high is to mountain.

7. _____ are to hands as toes are to feet.

8. Key is to door as combination is to _____.

9. Sapphire is to _____ as emerald is to green.

10. Aisle is to _____ as path is to woods.

11. Violin is to bow as piano is to _____.

12. Cheese is to mouse as acorn is to _____.

13. Barn is to _____ as coop is to chickens.

14. Freeze is to froze as _____ is to stood.

15. Rain is to monsoon as wind is to _____.

trout

canyon

blue

car

addition

squirrel

tornado

keys

stand

cows

safe

train

fingers

store

tropics

21

© Rainbow Bridge Publishing

Summer Bridge Reading RB-904094

Do They Agree?

Read each pair of words. Circle the word that belongs in the blank.

1. Sleep is to bed as mail is to _____.

   motor   letter   nurse

2. Dim is to bright as weak is to _____.

   strong   loose   dangerous

3. Creek is to brook as _____ is to path.

   trail   garden   bridge

4. Rabbit is to bunny as _____ is to calf.

   horse   bird   cow

5. Slick is to slippery as _____ is to fast.

   swift   slow   old

6. Bed is to boy as _____ is to baby.

   feather   dentist   cradle

7. Steel is to car as _____ is to house.

   brass   wood   silver

8. Poodle is to dog as _____ is to bird.

   lion   spider   sparrow

9. Niece is to nephew as sister is to _____ .

   brother   cousin   father

10. Apple is to fruit as _____ is to vegetable.

    plum   juice   corn

Almost Late

> Putting a series of events in a logical order is called **sequencing**.

The sentences in the paragraphs are out of order. Rewrite each paragraph so that it makes sense.

1. Charlie had to run to catch the school bus. If he had eaten breakfast at home, he would have had a three-mile walk to school. The alarm did not go off in the Cole house, and everyone overslept. When Charlie found a seat and sat down, he ate the apple that he had grabbed on his way out the door.

_____

_____

_____

_____

_____

_____

2. It was Field Day. Charlie was wearing a green shirt because he was on the green team. That meant the entire school was divided into six teams: red, white, blue, green, yellow, and orange. Charlie was glad to be on the bus, because today was a special day at school.

Flower Pressing

The following sentences are out or order. Number the sentences in a sensible order that explains how to press flowers.

_____ Pansies, violets, small grass flowers, and petunias are the best flowers for pressing. Pick them when they are at their prettiest.

_____ Before you find flowers, make sure that you have everything else you need.

_____ Place a thick layer of newspaper over the tissue.

_____ Then, find flowers or leaves that are good for pressing.

_____ Put several heavy books on top of the newspaper.

_____ Leave the tissue, newspaper, and books this way for 24 hours.

_____ Lay the flowers flat between two layers of facial tissue.

_____ Replace the tissue and put the newspaper and books back for another 24 hours to ensure that the flowers will dry.

_____ After 24 hours, carefully remove the books, newspaper, and tissue.

Now that you know how to make pressed flowers, use them to make a floral picture. Read the mixed-up directions below and number them in a logical order.

_____ First, cut out two circles from different colors of construction paper. Make one circle a little larger than the other.

_____ Finally, put a ribbon through the hole, tie it in a loop, and hang the floral picture.

_____ With the circles ready, use tweezers to arrange the pressed flowers in a nice arrangement and glue them into place.

_____ Next, glue the small circle on top of the larger one.

_____ You will need scissors, tweezers, a paper hole punch, ribbon, white glue, construction paper, and pressed flowers.

_____ Then, punch a hole on the outer rim of the joined circles.

Emma's Job

Read the passage.

My name is Emma. I am an editor at a publishing house. My job is to find great children's stories and help them get published as books that you can buy in a store or check out at the library. I love my job. Let me tell you all about it.

Many people send me their ideas for books. Some of the ideas are not very good, some are OK, and some are great. I look for the ones that I think are great and that I think kids would love to read. If I like an author's idea, I ask her to send me a copy of her story.

Authors get ideas for stories in many ways. Some write about imaginary things. Others write about things that actually happened. Authors can tell a story just like it really happened, or they can change the events to make the story more interesting. As they write, authors try to think of the right words to tell the story. They might make lists of words, take notes, or make outlines. Sometimes, authors need more information to write. They may go to the library, take field trips, or look up their topics on the Internet. When they write, authors change words that don't sound right.

When the author is finished writing the story, she sends a copy of it to me. If I like it, I call the author and offer to publish her story. Then, I read the story again. I give the author suggestions for making the story even better. I tell the author what I really like, and I may recommend some better words. Many people read the book and offer suggestions for making it better. The author rewrites the story until it is just right.

When the book is finished, I work with a designer to plan how the book will look. We choose the size of the book, the font, and the style of pictures that will match the story. The designer hires an artist to draw the pictures. The artist does not talk to the author.

When everything is ready, I send the pictures and story to the printer. The printer and binder put all of the pieces together and ship the finished books to our warehouse. From the warehouse, we ship the books to stores and libraries around the world. I know that you are a writer, too. Does some of the work I do look like the work you do when you write? Maybe someday, you will send me one of your stories.

Emma's Job

1. Put the steps of the publishing process in order from 1–12.

_____ The editor helps the author rewrite the story.

_____ The author gets an idea.

_____ The printer and binder put the book together.

_____ The editor offers to publish the story.

_____ The artist draws the pictures.

_____ The editor plans what the book will look like with the designer.

_____ The author writes a story.

_____ The designer hires an artist.

_____ The author sends the story to the editor.

_____ The books are shipped around the world.

_____ The author rewrites the story until it is just right.

_____ You buy the book in a bookstore.

2. Think about the process you go through when you write. Write the steps you take in your writing process.

_____

_____

_____

3. Which of the steps in your writing process are just like the steps in publishing a book?

_____

_____

_____

Mapping It Out

> Unlike stories, **directions** have no plot. Instead, they help the reader do something or get somewhere. The steps in directions should be read one at a time and followed exactly. It may be easy to lose your place or skip important parts. To prevent this, be sure to check off the directions as you complete them.

On his way to work, Trey's father drops Trey off at school each morning. To avoid traffic, they take many different streets and avenues. Look at the map and read the directions. Then, trace the route that Trey and his father take each morning.

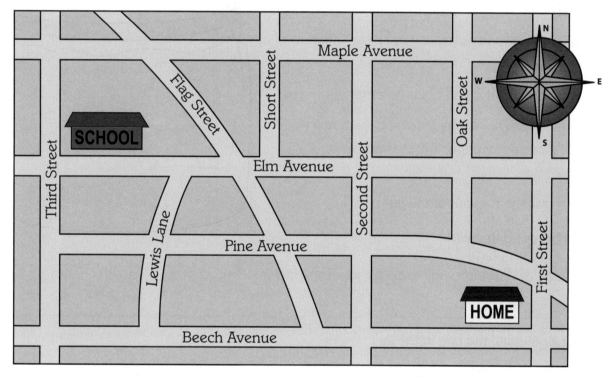

1. When Trey and his father leave their house each the morning, they head north on First Street.

2. They make a left turn at the first intersection that they reach. They are now heading west.

3. They turn right onto the next street that is not named after a type of tree.

4. Trey and his father turn west onto Maple Avenue.

5. They turn left at the second intersection that they reach. Now, they are heading southeast.

6. Trey and his father make a left turn at Elm Avenue, and Trey's father drops him off in front of the school.

Air Pressure

What is air pressure? Can you feel the pressure of the air around you? This experiment will help you see and feel air pressure. Read the directions and answer each question.

Materials:

- widemouthed jar or drinking glass
- plastic sandwich bag or empty bread bag
- thick rubber band

Directions:

1. Push a plastic sandwich bag deep into a jar so that it lines the jar.

2. Fold the top of the bag over the edge of the jar.

3. Make an airtight seal by placing a thick rubber band around the edge of the jar on the plastic bag.

4. Try to pull the bag out of the jar.

Answer the questions.

A. Is it easy or difficult to pull the bag out of the jar?

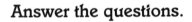

B. What is keeping the bag in the jar?

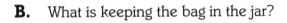

C. What do you see? Draw a picture in the box.

Antonio's Lizards

Read the story.

"Put on your coat!" Antonio's mother called as he went out the back door to shoot some baskets. "It's not as warm as it was last week."

"I already put it on," Antonio said. He didn't like it when his mother nagged him about wearing his coat, but he had to admit that she was right. His cousins in Ohio thought that Los Angeles was warm in February, but they were wrong. The cold wind made his face tingle.

He started with his sweet shot, the one he could make with his eyes closed. He aimed for the backboard, but he was out of practice. The ball bounced off the rim and landed in the dirt beside the garage.

He picked it up. He was about to go back and try the shot again when he spotted the first fence lizard. It was sitting at the edge of the cement driveway trying to soak up a little bit of warmth. It didn't even run away when he got close.

The weather had played a mean trick on the lizard. First, it was as warm as spring, so the lizard came out of its hole to find something to eat. When it turned cold again, the lizard didn't even have the energy to walk back home. Antonio was afraid that his ball would crush the little fellow.

Suddenly, he remembered that an old aquarium was in his closet. It had been empty since last summer. He went into the family room. His father was watching a basketball game. Antonio told him about the lizard. Together, they chose a small paper bag from the recycling bins in the cupboard. Antonio almost hoped that the lizard would be gone when they got back to the spot by the driveway, but it was still there.

Gently, Antonio's dad picked up the lizard and put it in the bag. Antonio picked up some dirt, sticks, and leaves to put in the bottom of the aquarium so that his little friend would feel at home. His dad put the aquarium on top of Antonio's dresser.

Antonio went outside to shoot some more baskets. He made two shots. When he missed the next one, he found two more lizards. By the end of the day, he had four lizards in the aquarium. He kept them until the weather was warm again. Then, he and his dad took them back outside. They let them go.

Summer Bridge Reading RB-904094

Antonio's Lizards

Answer the following questions.

1. Who is the main character in this story?

   _____

2. What problem does the main character have to solve?

   _____

3. How does the main character solve the problem?

   _____

4. Who helps the main character?

   _____

5. In what city does the story take place?

   _____

6. In what season does the story take place?

   _____

7. In what month does the story take place?

   _____

Extra! Write a story that takes place in your town in July.

   _____

   _____

   _____

   _____

   _____

   _____

   _____

   _____

Field Trip

Read the story.

Every year, the fifth graders at Brookstone Elementary go on a field trip to Toronto, Canada. Rob Kolbe has heard about the trip from his fifth-grade friends. He knows that they will visit the CN Tower, Casa Loma, and the Ontario Science Centre. Rob is really looking forward to going next year, but his mom and dad cannot afford to pay for the whole trip.

Rob asks his mom and dad whether they will pay for half of the trip if he earns the other half of the money himself. His parents agree, and Rob has almost a year to earn $150.

The holiday season is coming soon, and Rob decides to earn money babysitting. He types a nice letter and places his picture on it. The letter states that he will babysit while his neighbors do their holiday shopping. He will babysit any kids between the ages of three and seven at his house. He lists a few afternoons and a Friday evening when he can babysit because his mom or dad will be home. He gives the hours and says that it will cost $1 per hour per child. When the kids come, Rob plays games with them. After five babysitting sessions, Rob has $45.

When the warm weather arrives, Rob knocks on his neighbors' doors to ask if they need help with yard work. He helps mow lawns and rake leaves. He also weeds gardens. When the summer ends, Rob has $75 more from helping with yard work.

Rob spends a little of the money he earned. When fall arrives, Rob counts his money and determines that he still needs $40 for his trip. Rob's mom sees an advertisement for a job that Rob could do. He gets the job of delivering newspapers every Wednesday afternoon. He makes 5¢ for every paper that he delivers. Each Wednesday, he earns $10.

It isn't long before Rob has enough money to go on the trip to Toronto. He is just in time. The class trip is on October 15.

Rob's mom and dad give him a check for the $150 they promised him. Rob withdraws his money from the bank and brings all of the money to school. What a great feeling! Rob helped pay for his trip. He cannot wait to go.

Field Trip

Answer the following questions.

1. Who are the characters mentioned in the story?

    _____

2. Who is the main character?

    _____

3. Write a sentence that describes the main character.

    _____

4. What is the problem in the story?

    _____

5. What solution does the main character propose?

    _____

6. What are the steps that he takes to solve the problem?

    _____

7. Does he reach his goal?

    _____

8. How does the main character feel about the solution to the problem?

    _____

9. If you were Rob, what would you have done?

    _____

Summer Bridge Reading RB-904094

The Five Ws

> As you read, ask yourself the **five Ws**: Who? What? When? Where? Why? Asking yourself these questions will help you identify the important elements in a story.

Write the five Ws on the lines to identify the following story elements.

who	what	when	where	why

1. a 10-year-old boy

   _____

2. feels scared

   _____

3. on the dark road home

   _____

4. because he is alone

   _____

5. late at night

   _____

Use the story elements above to write a scary story.

_____

_____

_____

_____

_____

_____

Summer Bridge Reading RB-904094

Primates

The **main idea** tells what a passage is mostly about. The main idea in a paragraph is often stated in the first or second sentence and may be summed up in the final sentence.

Read the paragraphs. Underline the sentence in each paragraph that tells its main idea.

One reason to classify animals is to determine which are related to each other. Usually, such classification is achieved by studying the skeletons and skins of the animals. Have you ever wondered to which animals you are related?

Monkeys and apes belong to a group called primates. (The word *primate* comes from a Latin word that means *first*.) Monkeys and apes are called primates because they have complex brains. They are the most intelligent of all animals. Human beings are also classified as primates. Monkeys and apes have large brains like we do, and they use the ends of their front limbs as hands. Monkeys, apes, and humans can think and use tools.

One type of primate, the chimpanzee, eats mostly fruits. However, it also will eat vegetables. It has even been seen eating insects and small animals. Chimpanzees use sticks to get honey from a honeycomb or to dig ants and termites from their nests.

What's in a Name?

Read each paragraph. Then, circle the letter next to the sentence that gives the main idea.

1. Amber Wilson hated her name. Without even trying, she could think of 20 better names. In fact, when her family moved to Lakeville, she thought about telling everybody that her name was Madison. She decided that it wasn't a good idea. She might not turn around when someone said, "Madison." She hated the name *Amber*, but she was used to it.

   A. Amber thought of 20 other names.

   B. Amber Wilson hated her name.

2. Then, Amber read a chapter about gems in her science book. She learned that pieces of amber were fossils, like dinosaur bones. They started out as sap. Trees with layers of sap on their trunks aged and died. When they fell down, they were covered with dirt or water. The trees were buried for millions of years, and lumps of dry, hard sap became amber.

   A. Amber comes from sap.

   B. Trees were buried.

3. She found out that some pieces of amber have bugs or parts of plants in them. Long ago, in a prehistoric forest, insects landed on the sticky sap. They couldn't get away. Another layer of sap oozed down on top of them. It preserved them. Some of those bugs were alive during the age of dinosaurs.

   A. Insects were covered by sap.

   B. Some pieces of amber have bugs or parts of plants in them.

Extra! Everyone in Amber's class read the chapter. They all wanted to be named after a gem, especially one with bugs inside from the age of dinosaurs. Do you like your name? Why or why not?

_____

_____

_____

© Rainbow Bridge Publishing

Kenyon's Finch

Read each paragraph. Circle the letter next to the sentence that tells the main idea.

1. One morning, a bird flew up on Kenyon's front porch. It had a twig in its beak. It put the twig in a space under the porch roof. Then, it flew away. Kenyon looked up the bird in a book. It was a female house finch. The next day, the finch came back. She had a piece of grass this time. Kenyon was excited. He knew that the finch was building a nest. He could hardly wait to see the baby finches.

   A. Kenyon saw a bird fly up on his porch.

   B. A finch was building her nest on Kenyon's porch.

   C. The bird came back again and again.

2. Kenyon and his family did not use the front door for the next few weeks. They did not want to bother the bird. When the nest was finished, the finch sat in it most of the time. Kenyon knew that she was sitting on her eggs. Two weeks later, Kenyon went to the front window to look at the finch as usual. The finch was not there. Kenyon stayed to watch. Soon, the finch came flying back. Kenyon looked very carefully. He saw five little beaks. The mother finch put food in every beak. Then, she flew away again. Kenyon ran to tell everyone. The baby finches had hatched!

   A. After two weeks, the baby finches hatched.

   B. Kenyon's family did not use the front door.

   C. The finch sat on her eggs to keep them warm.

3. Kenyon made a feeder for the finch family. He found a book in the library about making things out of wood. He read all of the directions. He made a pattern. Then, he made a list of the materials that he would need. His dad drove him to the local building supply store. They found everything on Kenyon's list. Kenyon traced his pattern on the wood. His older brother cut the wood with a saw. Kenyon sanded and painted the bird feeder by himself. He hung it outside in a tree beside the porch. Kenyon was proud when he saw the little finches at his feeder.

   A. Kenyon has a big brother.

   B. Kenyon makes many things out of wood.

   C. Kenyon made a bird feeder.

Insfrom

Insects

Read the passage. Underline the sentence in each paragraph that tells the main idea.

Insects are truly amazing animals. They come in beautiful colors and a variety of interesting shapes. Insects are almost everywhere! They live in cold and hot climates. They live in wet jungles and dry deserts. They can live underground and high in the trees. There are at least one million different species of insects, and every year, new species are discovered.

Insects do many of the same things that humans do, but they do them in unique ways. Insects can hear, but some insects hear with hairs that cover their bodies. Other insects have hearing organs on their legs or hear from the sides of their bodies. Some insects smell with their antennae. Others taste with their feet.

Some insects are beneficial to humans. Bees make honey. Bees, wasps, butterflies, and other insects pollinate flowers and other plants. Some fruits and vegetables would not produce seeds if bees, wasps, butterflies and other insects did not pollinate them. Some insects eat or destroy pests that ruin our crops. Insects are also an important part of many animals' diets. Birds, fish, and frogs eat insects. Some insects even taste good to people!

Some insects are harmful to humans. There are insects that eat crops. Other insects get into our homes and destroy our clothes, books, and stored foods. Termites can be serious pests when they chew the wood frames of buildings! Worst of all, some insects carry diseases that can make people very sick.

Although all insects have six legs, three body parts, and two antennae, each species of insects is unique. Insects can be beautiful or ugly, helpful or harmful, or noisy or quiet. With all of that variety, insects help make the world a very interesting place.

37

Aesop's Fables

Usually, the main idea in a story or passage is stated at the beginning. There are times when it is stated at the end. Aesop's Fables are examples of this. They tell stories to illustrate lessons or morals. The ends of the stories usually wrap up or summarize the lessons.

Read the synopsis of each fable. Circle the letter next to the moral that summarizes each story.

The Hare and the Tortoise

One day, a hare was making fun of a tortoise and called him a slowpoke. That made the tortoise mad, so he challenged the hare to a race. Of course, the hare knew that he would win. When the hare was far enough ahead, he stopped for a rest and fell asleep. The tortoise plodded along, never stopping. When the hare woke up, he ran as fast as he could to the finish line. However, the tortoise had already crossed it. The moral of the story is . . .

1. A. a lazy hare is fast.

   B. do not brag or boast.

   C. the slow turtle wins.

The Fox and the Crow

A crow sat in a tree with a piece of cheese that she had just taken from an open window. A fox who was walking by saw the crow and wanted the cheese. The fox complimented the crow in many ways. The fox told the crow how nicely she sang. To prove her voice, the crow opened her mouth to sing. The cheese fell out, and the fox gobbled it up. The moral of the story is . . .

2. A. do not let flattery go to your head.

   B. listen before you sing.

   C. eat fast so that you will not lose your dinner.

The Dog and the Bone

A dog was walking over a bridge while carrying a bone. The dog looked into the stream and saw another dog carrying a bigger bone. The dog on the bridge jumped into the water because he wanted the bigger bone. But, he dropped his bone, and there was no other bone. The moral of the story is . . .

3. A. he lost his bone.

   B. the dog was wet.

   C. think before you act.

Mike and Moe

> An author includes many **details** to help the reader better understand a story. Details provide the reader with a clearer picture of the story elements, such as characters, setting, and plot.

Read the story and answer the questions.

We chose our first cat, Mike, at the animal shelter when he was only eight weeks old. He is white with orange stripes. He was a very independent kitten from the beginning. He came to us when he wanted to be with people, and he stayed in the area set aside for him in the basement when he was happy being alone. Mike grew to be a big cat, and he ruled our house.

When Mike was about two years old, I heard a faint cry while I was reading on the patio. I looked around in the shrubbery, under the furniture, and on the brick wall around the patio, but I did not see a thing. The crying persisted. Finally, about three feet above where I was sitting, I saw a tiny kitten hanging from a tree branch.

I called for my brother, Ben, to bring a ladder. Together, we leaned it against the tree. I held the ladder while Ben climbed up the first two rungs and reached for the kitten. Ben gently pulled it from the branch and handed me the tiniest kitten that I had ever seen.

We took the kitten to our veterinarian. She said that the kitten was probably about four weeks old. She told us how to feed him a special formula with an eyedropper. Ben and I fed the kitten this way for two weeks before he could drink from a saucer. As the kitten gained weight, he looked more and more like Mike. We named him Moe.

At first, Mike was not nice to Moe. Then, he learned to ignore Moe. Now, they are good friends. Moe is half of Mike's size and is scared of his own shadow. We have no idea how Moe ended up in that tree, but we are glad that he did. We think Mike is, too.

1. How high did Ben climb on the ladder? _____

2. When did Moe come to the house? _____

3. How many places were searched before Moe was found? _____

4. What adjective was used to describe Mike as an individualist? _____

5. Describe Mike as a grown cat. _____

6. How long did Moe have to be fed with a dropper? _____

7. What was the author doing when he heard Moe's cry? _____

8. Where did the author's family get Mike? _____

You probably already know many traffic rules. Review the traffic rules. Then, use them to answer the following questions.

- Never run into the street. Stop at the curb or by the edge of the road.
- Always look left, right, and left again before crossing the street. Check to see if a vehicle is coming around the corner.
- Use your ears as well as your eyes. If you hear sirens, move out of the path of traffic immediately.
- Obey all traffic signs and signals. Do not speed up to cross during a yellow light.
- Cross on crosswalks or at corners.
- Never cross between parked cars.
- Watch out for cars backing out of driveways.
- Do not play in the street or in parking lots.
- Walk on sidewalks whenever they are available. If there are no sidewalks, walk on the left side of the road facing traffic.
- When crossing a street, walk quickly. Do not run, because you could fall. Do not walk slowly, because a vehicle that was not there when you last looked may be coming.
- If you have to walk through busy traffic areas, plan your route ahead of time.
- If you have to walk outside after dark, carry a flashlight and wear bright, colorful clothing.

1. What should you do before crossing a street? _____

_____

2. What are three ways not to cross a street?_____

_____

3. Where is the best place to cross a street? _____

_____

4. What should you do when you are walking outside at night? _____

_____

5. If there are no sidewalks, where should you walk?_____

_____

The Saguaro Cactus

Read the passage.

In the Arizona desert, there is a cactus that will live 100 years or more. The saguaro cactus grows very slowly in the hot, dry desert, and it becomes home to many animals as it grows.

The cactus starts as a seed that is dropped from the fruit of a mature saguaro cactus. The seed sprouts after receiving moisture from a rare rain. The seed swells up, splits its shell, and sends a root into the desert soil. The seed sends up a stem that is green, moist, and covered with prickles.

It does not rain often in the desert, so the stem grows slowly. During its first year, it grows less than 0.39 inches (1 cm). After 10 years, it may be only 6 inches (15 cm) tall. When it is 50 years old, the original stem is about 15 feet (4.5 m) high. After 50 years, the saguaro cactus grows its first branches. The branches are moist and prickly, like the trunk. Over the next 50 years, the cactus may grow as tall as 35 feet (10.5 m).

Many animals make their homes in saguaro cacti. They like the moist skin of the cacti. A woodpecker may build a deep nest in the side of a saguaro stem and lay its eggs there. After the eggs hatch, the baby birds eat insects that live on the cactus. Mice, hawks, and owls may also use the nest built by the woodpecker.

Beautiful flowers grow on the mature saguaro cactus. The flowers provide juicy nectar for birds, insects, and bats.

After the flowers dry up, green fruit covers the cactus. The fruit is sweet and juicy. Many animals come to eat the fruit. They spread the seeds from the fruit onto the ground, where the seeds wait for rain. Eventually, these seeds will sprout and grow new saguaro cacti.

Summer Bridge Reading RB-904094

The Saguaro Cactus

Draw the stages of the saguaro cactus life cycle. Label the pictures using the words in the box.

50 years	flowers	seed sprouts	animal homes	fruit	100 years

(Start here.)

SAGUARO CACTUS LIFE CYCLE

Compost Pile

Read the passage.

Do you throw away all of your garbage? Not everything that you throw away is trash. Some garbage can be recycled, and some can be composted. A compost pile is a pile of leaves, grass, and some kinds of leftover foods that is kept outside.

It is not difficult to make a compost pile. All you need is a small corner of your yard in which you can make a pile. Some people keep their compost in large, wooden boxes without lids. Other people buy special bins that turn or mix the compost for them. A compost container is mostly filled with shredded newspaper, grass, and leaves. People also put apple peelings, eggshells, and vegetable ends in compost piles. Meat scraps should not be added to a compost pile, because they do not decompose fast enough and may attract unwanted animals.

Take care of your compost pile. It can start to smell bad if you do not stir it. If you remember to stir your compost, the pile will not get bigger, even if you keep adding things to it. A compost pile can work in two different ways: the sunshine and water help the leaves, grass, and leftovers rot, or little, red worms eat the compost. In worm composting, worms eat the compost materials and their bodies turn the food into rich soil.

A compost pile helps you in many ways. You throw away less garbage each week. That means garbage dumps fill more slowly. A compost pile also makes very good natural fertilizer for your yard, garden, and houseplants. A compost pile is a fun science experiment, too. You will be amazed how quickly the pile of material gets smaller and by how many critters live there.

...e letter next to the main idea of each paragraph. Then, list three details
...port the main idea.

1. What is the main idea of the first paragraph?

   A. You should throw away garbage.   **B.** A compost pile is kept outside.

   C. Not everything that you throw away   **D.** Some garbage can be recycled.
      is trash.

Write three details that support the main idea.

_____

_____

2. What is the main idea of the second paragraph?

   A. A compost pile is simple to make.   **B.** You have to buy a special bin.

   C. You can make compost in your yard.   **D.** Some compost bins do not have lids.

Write three details that support the main idea.

_____

_____

3. What is the main idea of the third paragraph?

   A. Compost is a great fertilizer.   **B.** Compost can smell bad.

   C. You must take care of your compost pile.   **D.** Compost piles work in two different ways.

Write three details that support the main idea.

_____

_____

4. What is the main idea of the fourth paragraph?

   A. Critters love compost.   **B.** A compost pile helps you.

   C. A compost pile is not expensive.   **D.** A compost pile is a fun science experiment.

Write three details that support the main idea.

_____

_____

Planet Earth

Read each sentence. If the sentence tells how Earth is the same as the moon, write *same*. If it tells how Earth is different, write *different*.

1. There are oceans on Earth, but there is no water on the moon. _____

2. People live on Earth, but no one lives on the moon. _____

3. Earth is shaped like a ball, and the moon is, also. _____

4. The gravity of Earth pulls on the moon, and the gravity of the moon pulls on Earth.

_____

5. There are many plants and animals on Earth, but there are none on the moon.

_____

6. A day lasts 24 hours on Earth, but it lasts about 720 hours on the moon.

_____

Extra! Write a story about taking a trip to a colony on the moon. Look up *moon* in the encyclopedia to find more details for your story.

Summer Bridge Reading RB-904094

nic was one of the finest ships ever built. It was designed to be comfortable *irious*. It was like a floating palace. Read the passage to discover what life was like on this expensive ship that made only one voyage.

There were three levels of tickets. The most expensive tickets were first class. The next level was second class. The least expensive tickets were for people traveling in third class, or steerage.

The 329 first-class passengers had four decks on which to move around. They could visit with friends in the sitting rooms of their cabins and in several different lounges, restaurants, and dining rooms. They had a gym, a pool, a Turkish bath, a library, and beautiful, sunny decks. Their meals were made from the fanciest and most expensive foods, such as mutton chops, chicken galantine, and apple meringue. Dinners consisted of many courses, and first-class passengers could choose their meals from a menu. They ate at tables decorated with china plates, crystal, and fresh flowers. Some people in first class wrote about what the ship was like. It was even fancier than what most wealthy people had at home.

The 285 second-class passengers were treated how first-class passengers on other ships were treated. Their cabins were nice, but small. They ate a four-course meal each evening at nice tables with pretty plates. Like first class passengers, they could go on deck to walk around or sit in the sun. Their decks were smaller, however, because they held the lifeboats. Second class also did not have the restaurants, gyms, and other special rooms that the first class passengers had.

The 710 third-class passengers had space in the noisy rear of the ship below second class. There were only 220 cabins in steerage. Families used these cabins. The other passengers slept in large rooms. The men slept in one room, and the women slept in another room. The steerage sitting room was a large, plain room with benches and tables. Third-class passengers had to take turns eating in a dining room that sat only 473 people at a time. Tickets told them when to eat. If they missed their times, passengers went hungry until the next meal. There were no restaurants for them.

Most of the passengers knew that they were on a special trip. The *Titanic* was supposed to be the finest ship ever built. Some very rich and famous people were on the ship for its first trip. Of course, no one on board knew that the boat would sink. This fact probably made the *Titanic*'s first and only trip across the ocean the most famous voyage of all time.

Answer the following questions using complete sentences.

1. How did meals in first class differ from meals in second class?

_____

_____

_____

2. What was in the first-class cabins that was not in the second- or third-class cabins?

_____

3. How did the sleeping rooms in third class compare to the ones in first and second class?

_____

_____

4. What did most passengers know about this trip?

_____

Read the words below of each passenger. Write *1* if the passenger who is speaking traveled first class on the *Titanic*, *2* if the passenger traveled second class, and *3* if the passenger traveled third class.

_____   "I love my room. I have a beautiful bedroom with a private sitting room."

_____   "My favorite meal is dinner, when we have a delicious four-course meal."

_____   "We swam for hours in the pool this afternoon."

_____   "In the evening, we sit on benches in the only room that we all share. We play music and dance."

_____   "I love to sit on the deck in the sun. My brother likes to play under the lifeboats."

_____   "We had a nice meal. We had to eat a little fast so that the next group of people could eat."

© Rainbow Bridge Publishing

Summer Bridge Reading RB-904094

Whales

Read the passage.

There are many different kinds of whales. Whales are not fish; they are mammals. They swim in the water but breathe air. Whales breathe through the blowholes on the tops of their heads. They have smooth skin that allows them to move quickly in water. Whales use their strong tails to push themselves forward. They have thick layers of blubber under their skin that keep them warm. There are two main groups of whales: baleen whales and tooth whales.

Baleen whales do not have teeth. Instead, they have a baleen that they use to strain their food. The baleen is made up of hard, comblike plates that hang down from the whale's upper jaw. When it wants to eat, the baleen whale swims through the water with its mouth open. Then, it closes its mouth, the water rushes out, and the tiny animals are trapped inside.

Blue whales are one type of baleen whale. Blue whales are not only the largest whales, they are also the largest animals that have ever lived. A blue whale can grow to be nearly 100 feet (30 m) long. The blue whale's tongue alone can weigh as much as an elephant.

The blue whale likes to eat krill, which are tiny shrimp. Krill live in cold water, so blue whales spend their summers near the North and South Poles. They spend their winters in warmer water, where there are fewer krill. When there are not many krill, blue whales live off of the blubber that they have stored in their bodies.

Unlike baleen whales, toothed whales have teeth and eat fish, squid, and other sea animals. Sperm whales are one type of toothed whale. Sperm whales can grow to be 70 feet (20 m) long. A sperm whale has the largest brain of any animal. Its brain is about the size of a basketball and weighs more than 15 pounds (7 kg).

The sperm whale is strong and powerful and likes to eat squid. Sperm whales live around the world, but they usually stay away from the coldest waters near the North and South Poles. Sperm whales have large heads that are filled with a waxy substance called spermaceti. The spermaceti might help the whales float.

For hundreds of years, people have hunted whales for their meat and blubber. Hunters have sold the parts of whales for money. The blue whale's baleen was once sold to make jewelry. The sperm whale's spermaceti was sold to make candles and makeup. Some whales were becoming endangered because of hunting. Now, whale hunting is against the law in most countries.

Whales

Complete the Venn diagram with the characteristics of blue whales and sperm whales listed in the box.

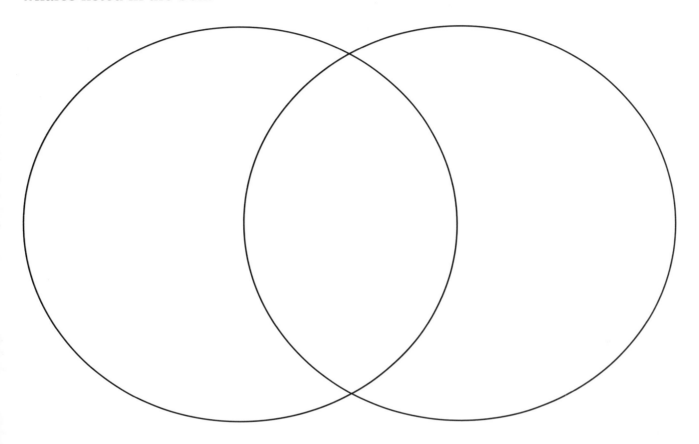

baleen whale

breathe through blowholes

largest brain of any animal

stay away from North and South Poles

spend summers near North and South Poles

hunted for meat and blubber

mammals

strain food

smooth skin

eat krill and live off blubber in winter

hunted for spermaceti

toothed whale

largest whale

layer of blubber under skin

eat fish, squid, and other sea animals

hunted for baleen

Why Did That Happen?

> There are times when one thing causes another thing to happen. This is a cause-and-effect relationship. The **cause** is the reason, and the **effect** is the result.
> **Example:** April showers bring May flowers.
>   "April showers" is the cause. "Bring May flowers" is the effect.

Causes are on the left. Effects are on the right. Write the letter of the effect on the line after its cause.

1. After a week of rain, _____

2. When the car came to a sudden stop, _____

3. My bike hit a rock in the road, _____

4. With a minute left, we scored a goal _____

5. In chemistry class, we mixed the two chemicals and _____

6. After the drive on the dusty dirt roads, _____

7. There was a loud crash outside, _____

8. I heard the bell ring _____

9. When the dog heard the thunder, _____

10. It would soon be dark enough _____

11. We went to the airport _____

12. The team practiced every day _____

13. Once the lawn mower motor started, _____

14. On Saturday, my dad tripped on the doormat _____

15. The mail carrier rang our bell _____

A. and broke his ankle.

B. smoke filled the laboratory.

C. to shoot off fireworks.

D. to win the soccer game 5 to 4.

E. to pick up our guests.

F. the car needed a bath.

G. the river rose over its banks.

H. because he had a special-delivery letter.

I. the seat belt tightened.

J. so I ran to see what happened.

K. and it flew into the air with me still on it.

L. in preparation for the big game.

M. and ran the rest of the way to school.

N. he hid under the bed.

O. Father was able to cut the grass.

Sara's Day

Read each pair of sentences. Write *effect* on the line after each sentence that states an effect. Write *cause* on the line after each sentence that states a cause.

1. Sara watched a scary movie on television _____

    Sara could not sleep. _____

2. Sara was late for school. _____

    Sara woke up late. _____

3. Sara had to do her homework during recess. _____

    Sara forgot to bring her homework to school. _____

4. Sara left her lunch ticket at home. _____

    Sara had to wait in the lost-ticket line. _____

5. Sara had to answer history questions during P.E. _____

    Sara fell asleep during history class. _____

6. Sara felt better. _____

    On her way home, Sara told a friend about her bad day. _____

7. That night, Sara watched a comedy. _____

    Sara laughed. _____

8. She woke up right on time. _____

    Sara got a good night's sleep. _____

Extra! Read *If You Give a Mouse a Cookie* or *If You Give a Moose a Muffin* by Laura Joffe Numeroff. Look for examples of cause and effect in the story.

Read the passage.

Beavers are good swimmers. They are at home on land and underwater. They spend their lives around streams. They eat the soft, inner bark of trees and bushes that grow near water. They like to eat aspens, birches, and willows.

Many of the places where beavers live are very cold in the winter. Their dams help them create homes that are safe and comfortable in frigid weather.

Ice forms on top of a beaver pond, but the water underneath does not freeze. Maybe you have heard the saying "busy as a beaver." During the late summer and early fall, beavers are very busy, indeed. They store supplies of branches and sticks underwater. When winter arrives, they do not have to hibernate. They swim out under the ice to get the food that they have saved.

The beaver family builds a home, called a lodge, on the bank of a stream or in a shallow part of a pond. The entrance to the lodge is underwater, but the floor is above the waterline. The lodge has a roof made of sticks and branches. It stays dry and cozy all winter.

Read each pair of sentences. Draw a line from the sentence that states the cause to the word *cause*. Draw a line from the sentence that states the effect to the word *effect*.

1. A pond forms behind the dam.   cause

2. A beaver family builds a dam across a stream.   effect

3. Ice forms on top of the pond, but the water underneath does not freeze.   cause

4. The pond is deep.   effect

5. The floor of the lodge is above the waterline.   cause

6. The inside of the lodge is warm and dry.   effect

7. The entrance tunnels are underwater.   cause

8. Beavers can swim out under the ice.   effect

The Neighborhood Fort

Read the passage.

All of the kids in the neighborhood loved to play in the fort. The fort was a small, fenced-in area behind the empty house on the corner. The house had been empty and for sale for six months. Every day, kids played in the fort. Nobody could see them there. They played tag; they held court; they pretended that they were at school. Then, one day, someone bought the house.

The fort was a place that was not good for anything but a fort. One side was the back of the garage. The second side was the back of the deck. The third side was the side of the neighbor's garage. The fourth side was the back fence of the house on the next street. To get to the fort, the neighborhood kids had to walk between the side of the garage and the neighbor's fence. When the "Sold" sign was placed in front of the house, all of the kids wondered what would happen to their fort.

A new family moved into the house. They had little kids. That was promising. They were friendly people, but who would ask them about using the fort? Day after day, the fort was empty. The neighborhood kids played in their front yards together, but all that they talked about was the fort. They missed playing there, but they stayed away all summer.

When the kids went back to school in the fall, they talked more about the fort. "I think that we should ask the new neighbors if we can play there," said Alex. The kids agreed and sent Alex and Brian to knock on the door. When the door opened, Alex nervously asked, "May we play in the fort behind your house? We used to play there, and we will be careful."

"Well, I don't know," said the new owner, Mrs. Johnson. "Let's go back there together, and you can show me what you will do there. Then, we can talk about whether you may play there."

The neighborhood kids showed Mrs. Johnson the fort. They showed her how they got in and where they played. When they were finished explaining, Mrs. Johnson said, "OK. You may play here if you promise to play safely and quietly." That sounded fair to everyone, so they agreed.

Now, the neighborhood kids meet at the fort after school. They play tag, court, and school. They take good care of the fort and play quietly. Once in a while, they have little visitors from the Johnson house. The kids invite the little ones in, and they have tea parties. Mrs. Johnson supplies the tea and cookies.

The Neighborhood Fort

Answer the following questions using complete sentences.

1. What is the effect of the house being sold?

   _____

2. What causes the neighborhood kids to stay away from the fort?

   _____

3. What is the effect of the new neighbors moving into the house?

   _____

4. What causes the kids to knock on the Johnson's door?

   _____

5. What is the effect of the kids knocking on the Johnson's door?

   _____

6. What rules does Mrs. Johnson set into effect?

   _____

7. What is the cause for the kids having tea parties?

   _____

8. Do you think that the neighborhood kids are happy that the Johnsons moved in, or are they sad?

   _____

   Explain your answer. _____

   _____

9. Do you have a special place where you like to play? If so, describe the place. If not, think of a place where you would like to play. What is special about this place?

   _____

   _____

   _____

   _____

Summer Bridge Reading RB-904094

That's a Fact!

Read each sentence. Circle *fact* if the statement is a fact. Circle *opinion* if the statement is an opinion.

1. When Europeans came to the land that is now the United States, there were huge flocks of swans.   Fact   Opinion

2. Hunters killed the big, white birds for their feathers.   Fact   Opinion

3. After years of being hunted, most of the swans were gone.   Fact   Opinion

4. The bird artist John James Audubon drew with a swan feather.   Fact   Opinion

5. Swan feathers were better than metal pens for drawing.   Fact   Opinion

6. It was important to save these beautiful birds.   Fact   Opinion

7. The Red Rock Lakes National Wildlife Refuge was started in Montana.   Fact   Opinion

8. The swans could not be hunted.   Fact   Opinion

9. It is wonderful that swans are coming back.   Fact   Opinion

10. A boy swan is called a cob, and a girl swan is called a pen.   Fact   Opinion

11. The calls of trumpeter swans are not very pretty.   Fact   Opinion

12. Trumpeter swans are named for the sounds that they make.   Fact   Opinion

Is That a Fact?

Read each sentence. Circle *fact* if the statement is a fact. Circle *opinion* if the statement is an opinion.

1. Eric the Red was a Viking.   Fact   Opinion

2. Vikings were brave people.   Fact   Opinion

3. Vikings lived in lands that are now Norway, Sweden, and Denmark.   Fact   Opinion

4. There was not much good farmland in the cold north.   Fact   Opinion

5. Vikings sailed to distant lands.   Fact   Opinion

6. The Vikings built great ships.   Fact   Opinion

7. Eric the Red had red hair.   Fact   Opinion

8. Eric the Red settled Greenland.   Fact   Opinion

9. Greenland is a beautiful place to live.   Fact   Opinion

10. Eric the Red's son was Leif Erikson.   Fact   Opinion

Extra! Using the keyword *Viking*, search the Internet to find out more about these daring warriors.

What Makes You Think That?

Read each of the following situations. Then, explain why you think the characters make the choices that they do.

1. Felipe walked down a path in the woods on his way to a friend's house, and the path split. Felipe thought about which way to take. It was already late, and he was anxious to get to his friend's house. The path on the right was longer but easier to follow. The path on the left was shorter. However, overgrown bushes sometimes made this path difficult to follow. Felipe picked up a long stick and decided to take the path on the left.

Why do you think he decides that? _____

2. Grammy arrived for her usual summer visit. Everyone in our family was excited to see her. Eric, my seven-year-old brother, watched her unpack. He told her about receiving the reading award at school and what he had been doing since summer vacation had started. When she had everything put away, she handed Eric two packages and told him to choose one. He shook the small, square box wrapped in blue paper. Something inside the box rattled. The package wrapped in red paper with a ribbon was flat and heavier and did not make any noise when shaken. Eric decided on the latter package.

Why do you think he decides that?_____

3. Sometimes, my sister has a hard time figuring out what to wear. Today, she was going to an afternoon baseball game. It was supposed to be very hot, especially if she sat in the sun. There was a chance of rain, so she decided to take an umbrella. She was considering wearing either a dress without sleeves or long pants and a blouse. She might get too much sun in the dress, and she might be too hot in the pants and shirt. She decided to wear the dress.

Why do you think she decides that? _____

© Rainbow Bridge Publishing

Kick Ball

Read the passage.

By the time they got to the yard, the kids from Room 17 were already warming up. Austin's heart pounded. Rusty Stanford was pitching for the other team, and he was a good player.

"We'll flip a coin to see who's up first," said Mr. Armstrong, Room 17's teacher. "Let's have the two pitchers come over here."

Austin and Rusty faced each other at home plate. "Call it, Austin," Mr. Armstrong said.

"Aw, come on, Mr. Armstrong," Rusty said. The teacher glared at him. He did not say anything else.

"Tails," said Austin. Rusty grinned.

Mr. Armstrong tossed up the coin. It took what seemed like forever to Austin to come down. Mr. Armstrong caught the coin in his palm and slapped it down on the back of his hand. "Tails it is," he called out. "Room 15 is up first."

Rusty kicked the dirt beside the plate. "You may be up first, but you'll still lose," he said.

Austin was up first. Rusty's first pitch was high and bouncy. Austin stepped aside.

"Strike one," Mr. Armstrong called.

Rusty and Richard Susa, the first baseman, cheered. Rusty's second pitch was so slow that it hardly moved. Austin could have kicked it, but it wouldn't have gone very far.

"Strike two," Mr. Armstrong called.

"I told you that we'd win," said Rusty.

Rusty's third pitch was too bouncy, but it wasn't as high as the first one. It was Austin's last chance. He stepped back, ran to the plate, and kicked it high toward center field.

Write a conclusion to this story. Use a separate sheet of paper if necessary.

_____

_____

_____

_____

_____

Chris's Adventure

Read the passage.

Chris sat in the chair by the window. The grandfather clock at the bottom of the stairs started to chime. It echoed through the quiet halls.

Chris could hardly keep his eyes open. He knew that his pajamas were laid out neatly on the bed, but he did not want to put them on. If he had to run for help, he wanted to be wearing a shirt, jeans, and sneakers, not flannel pajamas with blue footballs all over them.

When his parents said that he could stay with his uncle while they were in France, he was happy. His other choice was Camp Blue Sky.

Chris hated Camp Blue Sky. At least at his uncle's house, he would have good food, a room of his own, and no leather crafts.

He closed his eyes and counted the clock's strikes—9, 10, 11, 12. He wished that he had chosen Camp Blue Sky. It was not perfect, but it was better than a spooky, old house.

The clock stopped chiming. The house was still. Chris opened his eyes and looked down on the garden. He wanted to see the mysterious light again. If he could tell what it was, he might be able to sleep.

At first, he saw nothing, just dark paths and the reflection of the half moon in a fish pond. Maybe the light that he saw the night before was just a dream.

Suddenly, he saw it again. At first, the white beam flickered. Then, it was steady. It moved across the far side of the garden just beyond the garage. When it came toward the house, Chris dove into bed.

He pulled the covers over his head and waited. His heart pounded. His bedroom door slowly creaked open. He tried to stay still, but he could not help shaking when a voice spoke his name.

59

Chris's Adventure

Read each pair of sentences. Circle the one that tells what probably happens next.

1. Chris flies to Camp Blue Sky.

Chris hears his uncle ask, "Are you all right?"

2. Chris pushes the covers back.

Chris becomes invisible.

3. Chris's uncle says that he went out to the shed to check on the rabbits.

Chris's uncle turns into a rabbit.

4. Chris's uncle is glowing.

Chris's uncle has a flashlight.

5. Chris's uncle takes him out to see the rabbits.

Chris's uncle tells him to clean the room.

6. Chris goes home.

Chris puts on his pajamas and goes to sleep.

Extra! Write your own ending to the story.

_____

_____

_____

_____

_____

A Camping Trip

Read the passage.

We started hiking on the trail early in the morning. The sun was rising in the sky, and the air around us was cold and misty. The pine trees looked like arrows that were pointing our way to the top of the mountain. It was a wonderful morning.

My mom and dad each carried a heavy backpack full of food, a tent, water, and other things. Ben and I carried packs, too. Mine had only my clothes and sleeping bag in it. I carried a few snacks in my pockets and two water bottles on my belt. Ben is stronger than I am, so he carried some food and a cookstove in his pack.

We walked quietly at first. My dad always says that you do not need words to be a part of the forest in the morning. I could hear birds singing and chipmunks moving through the leaves on the ground. There was no breeze, so the trees were silent. We walked single file along the trail.

At lunchtime, we stopped by a stream that flowed down the mountain. We could see a small waterfall higher up, but here, the water cut through the rocks and snaked past flowers and bushes. We took off our shoes and dipped our feet in the water. The sun shone brightly overhead, and we all took off our jackets.

I knew better than to ask how much farther we had to go. My parents always say that the hike itself is our destination. We would be walking for three days on these trails. We would see many beautiful sights and hear and smell things that we do not hear or smell in the city. At home, my mom and dad are teachers. Every summer, we take a trip as a family. Ben wanted to bring a friend this year, but my dad said that this was family time. Ben complained, but I know he likes family trips, too.

At dinnertime, we stopped and set up our tents on a flat meadow. We could see the next mountain peak from our site. It looked beautiful as the sun set behind it. We lit a fire and cooked dinner. We stayed awake a while longer to gaze at the stars. My mom pointed out several constellations. Someday, I want to be an astronomer.

We went to bed early because we were all tired from walking. Tomorrow, we will have another long walk. We will reach the top of the mountain. I have never stood on a mountaintop before. My dad said that I will be able to see forever. I think that I will like that. Maybe I will be able to see my friend Gena's house back home. I will wave to her and shout hello. I'll hear the echo and pretend that she shouted back at me. But, that is tomorrow, and my dad says that even the night is a part of the journey. So, I will close my eyes and listen for the owls, the wind in the trees, and the sound of my dad snoring. I love this place!

Answer the following questions.

1. Do you think that there is anyone else in the family who is not on the hike?

Explain your answer._____

2. How old do you think Ben is? _____

3. Do you know if the narrator is a boy or a girl?_____

4. Do you think that the narrator likes this trip? _____

Underline the sentences in the story that make you think that.

5. Where is the family hiking?_____

6. What time of year is it? _____

7. Has this family has been on a hike before? Explain your answer.

_____

8. What senses does the narrator use while hiking? _____

Give examples of what the narrator experiences with each sense. _____

_____

_____

_____

Circle the letters next to the sentences that the parents might say on this trip.

A. We will be there in one hour.

B. Do not rush.

C. I do not have all day!

D. Next time, you can stay home.

E. Turn up the music.

F. Getting there is half of the fun.

G. Listen. Did you hear that?

H. Take one step at a time.

The Junior Detectives

Read the passage.

Junior detective Jacob Wilson held a mirror in one hand and a Morse code book in the other. He was trying to figure out how to reflect sunlight with the mirror. He wanted to flash messages to his friend Matthew, who lived in the house across the street. He and Matthew got the idea from a spy movie they saw on television.

Jacob glanced over at Matthew's window. Something flashed. There were long flashes and short flashes. It was a message! Jacob wrote down a dash for each long flash and a dot for each short flash. When the flashing stopped, Jacob looked in his code book. The message was "C-o-m-e q-u-i-c-k."

Jacob climbed down the ladder. He wondered why Matthew wanted him to come over. The two of them did most of their detective club business up in the tree. It was more secret there.

When he knocked on the door to Matthew's room, his friend said, "Password?"

It took Jacob a minute to remember it. "Operation Reflect," he said.

The door opened. "It took you long enough," Matthew said.

Josh, a boy in their class, was sitting on Matthew's bed. Jacob waved to him and then made himself comfortable in the chair by Matthew's computer.

"So, what's going on?" Jacob asked.

"Josh has a new case for us," said Matthew. "It's a secret message. He found it when he got home from school."

Matthew handed Jacob a white pillowcase. The message was printed in pale blue ink. It was a group of strange symbols. It looked like this:

Friday Only: Two Pounds for the Price of One.

"What does it mean?" Jacob asked.

"We've been trying to figure it out for an hour," said Matthew.

Jacob spread the pillowcase out in his lap. He happened to look up and see his reflection in the mirror on Matthew's closet door.

"I have it!" he said.

He held the pillowcase up to the mirror. Matthew and Josh laughed.

"Somebody must have dropped some junk mail in the washing machine again," said Josh.

Hold this page up to a mirror. What does the message say?

_____

_____

The Junior Detectives

Circle the letter next to the best answer for each question.

1. What kind of a clubhouse do Jacob and Matthew have?

   A. a cave

   B. a tree house

   C. a shed

2. What symbols are used in Morse code?

   A. long and short dashes

   B. red, blue, and yellow beams of light

   C. patterns of shapes

3. What does each group of Morse code symbols stand for?

   A. a secret place

   B. an important person

   C. a letter of the alphabet

4. The word *reflection* comes from which of the following words?

   A. flecks

   B. reveal

   C. reflect

5. What must have happened while Josh was at school?

   A. Someone washed his pillowcase.

   B. His mom went shopping.

   C. His dog slept on the bed.

6. What kind of sale is the advertisement announcing?

   A. clothes

   B. shoes

   C. groceries

Extra! Find a Morse code key in the encyclopedia or online. Write a short message in dots and dashes. Trade messages with a friend.

The Shortcut

Read the story.

We should have taken the road home from the baseball park. It was getting dark, though, and we decided to take the shortcut home. I was the oldest and should have made a better choice. I did not know that there would be a train.

The shortcut from the baseball park to home was along the railroad tracks. After Reggie's game ended, we were excited. The game had gone into overtime, and Reggie's team had won! As we walked, Reggie and I gave each other high fives. Samantha and Brittany were chewing on their candy necklaces while they ran to keep up. When we came to the turn for the shortcut, we were so excited and happy that we just took it. We should have stayed on the road.

We walked for about five minutes on the tracks. The sides of the tracks were steep, and there were thick bushes and marshy water at the bottom. We stayed on the tracks. Samantha asked how we would know when a train was coming. I said that we would feel the tracks rumbling.

It was then that I heard the train whistle from far away. You can never tell when a train will come through. I did not want to worry the little ones, so I just said as calmly as I could, "Let's go back to the road." We turned around, and I walked pretty fast. Everyone followed.

Soon, we felt the tracks rumbling, and I shouted, "Run!" I grabbed Brittany in my arms, and Reggie held Samantha's hand. We ran as fast as we could. Then, I could see the headlights, and the train blew its loud whistle. We kept running, and I shouted, "Get off the tracks, now!" We jumped off the tracks. We all slid down the sides, trying hard to keep out of the scratchy bushes. Samantha and Brittany were crying, but I could not hear them. The loud train was rushing by us.

After the train went by, we climbed back up the hill. We were all scratched up from the bushes, but no one complained. We were all shaking as we walked back to the road. We did not have to talk. We all knew that we would never take the shortcut home again.

The Shortcut

Answer the following questions.

1. What bad decision do the children make?

_____

_____

2. In what way are the children brave?

_____

_____

3. In what way are the children careless?

_____

_____

4. Do you think that all of the children know that they are in danger when the train whistle blows the first time? _____

Why do you think that? _____

_____

5. Why are the children shaking as they walk back to the road?

_____

_____

6. Do you think that they will ever take the shortcut home again? _____

Why do you think that? _____

_____

66
Summer Bridge Reading RB-904094   © Rainbow Bridge Publishing

Read the passage.

Firefighters have a difficult but important job. They are highly trained, brave people who put out fires. They work hard to keep people from getting hurt in fires. They also try to prevent personal property from being damaged by fires. But, there are some fires that firefighters do not try to put out.

In 1972, a new policy concerning fire was written in the United States. The policy stated that if a fire is started by lightning in a national forest or park, it should not be put out unless it causes a threat to buildings, personal property, or the logging industry. Now, firefighters must decide whether a fire should be left to burn.

Fire is a natural part of the life cycle of a forest. About every 300 years, a natural fire can clean up a mature forest that is overgrown with underbrush and crowded with fallen trees. The fire can burn up the mess and make room for healthy, new growth. These natural fires usually burn themselves out on their own.

When there is a natural fire, firefighters watch it burn very carefully. They make sure that the fire does not get out of control. A strong wind can make a natural fire grow too large and threaten areas where people live or work.

Some forest fires are not started naturally. A careless person might throw down a burning cigarette in a forest and start a fire. Careless campers may let a campfire get out of control or not put it out properly. If one of these unnatural fires starts in the forest, firefighters will immediately work to put out the fire.

When firefighters must put out a large fire in a forest, they use many different methods. Firefighters use hoses and water from local lakes and streams to try to stop the flames. They may use axes to cut down trees that could burn and spread the fire. In some cases, they use bulldozers to push burnable materials away from the fire. Sometimes, airplanes drop chemicals on the fire. These chemicals slow down the fire. Another method is to light backfires. A backfire is a small, controlled fire that burns up the fuel (trees and shrubs) of a huge forest fire. Firefighters try to remove the materials that feed the fire with a backfire so that the fire will stop.

Firefighters

Answer the following questions using complete sentences.

1. What characteristics should a firefighter have?

   _____

   _____

2. When should a fire be left to burn?

   _____

   _____

3. What is a controlled fire?

   _____

   _____

4. Why would firefighters light a fire in order to put out a forest fire?

   _____

   _____

5. What does it mean to be brave?

   _____

   _____

6. What do firefighters watch for when they are allowing a forest fire to burn naturally?

   _____

   _____

7. How can a fire be good for a forest?

   _____

   _____

8. What does it mean to be careless?

   _____

   _____

What Do You Think?

> When you use **deductive reasoning**, you come to a logical conclusion based on information you already know.

Below are the endings for several stories. Circle what you think happens to cause the endings.

1. As disappointed as the fans were, they were good sports and served sandwiches to the visiting team before they left.

   A. The home team loses.

   B. Rain cancels the game.

   C. The fans cheer for their team.

   D. The home team wins.

2. Once the fire was under control, all but one of the fire engines left.

   A. A big fire starts in a field.

   B. Joe calls the police to report a robbery.

   C. A kitten climbs a tree and cannot get down.

   D. Some firefighters stay to make sure that the fire is completely out.

3. The kitten began to purr in the backseat as the Lees' car drove away from the animal shelter.

   A. The kitten walks happily around its new home.

   B. The kitten is hungry and tired.

   C. The kitten is adopted.

   D. The kitten is being tickled by Mrs. Lee.

4. The attendant at the gas station showed Dale the nail that had been taken from his tire.

   A. Dale buys a replacement tire.

   B. Dale has a flat tire.

   C. Dale is getting some gas at the filling station.

   D. Dale starts his car and heads home.

5. The crowd left after the President's limousine and all of the Secret Service cars drove away.

   A. There is a traffic jam.

   B. The President made a speech.

   C. The President is coming for a visit.

   D. The street is empty again.

6. The plows pushed the snow into large piles off the runway. Inside the airport, travelers waited impatiently to board their planes.

   A. The travelers have never seen snow before.

   B. All of the travelers like to fly.

   C. The travelers' flights have been delayed because of snow.

   D. It is the first snow of the season.

What's the Problem?

> **Analytical thinking** includes predicting outcomes, making inferences, drawing
> conclusions, and using deductive reasoning. These processes are similar in that their answers
> are not usually directly included in the reading material. It is up to the reader to figure out
> what the author means.

Read the following situations. Then, answer the questions.

1. Mr. Jones was driving on the highway on his way home from work when traffic began to slow down and came to a standstill. It took a half hour to travel one mile as traffic inched along. Drivers got out of their cars to see what the problem was, but they could not see it. It was too far away. Finally, Mr. Jones began to see orange barrels and cones blocking off one lane of the highway.

   What do you think the problem is? _____

   Why do you think this? _____

2. Mrs. Glass worked hard to clean her house to prepare for her luncheon. She ironed a tablecloth, polished the silver, and set out her best china. After setting the table, she went outside to pick some flowers for the centerpiece. When she went to the kitchen, she saw an empty platter. There had been cookies on it. She could not figure out who could have taken the cookies. Her dog would have made a mess, and her children were playing at their friend's house. The phone rang. It was her husband. He had forgotten his briefcase and had come home to get it.

   Who eats the cookies? _____

   Why do you think this? _____

3. Sam was about to play golf with his friends when he decided to get something to drink before they teed off. He went to the snack stand to buy some water. He set his golf bag by the door next to several others when he went inside. He was in a hurry, and as he left the store, he grabbed a bag without looking at it. When the golfers got to the green, Sam realized that the clubs he was carrying did not belong to him.

   How do you think Sam ends up with the wrong clubs? _____

   What makes you think this? _____

The Grass Is Always Greener

Read the passage and answer the questions.

Once upon a time, there was a princess named Priscilla. She had a normal infancy, but when she began to walk, her life changed. She was not allowed to go anywhere without being chaperoned by at least five royal guards. She wanted to play with other children her age, but her parents did not want her to go outside the castle walls.

One day, she escaped the guards' watchful eyes. She ran off into the forest. When she stopped running, she found herself amidst towering trees with hardly any sunlight filtering through their leafy branches. Squirrels ran from tree to tree, a deer raced by, and she heard unusual bird songs that she had never heard before. Suddenly, Priscilla realized that she did not know where she was or how to get home. She began to look for a familiar sight to help her find her way back to the castle.

At that moment, an ugly creature popped out from the shrubbery. He introduced himself as Whiz. He was a leprechaun who could grant Priscilla one wish. Priscilla did not hesitate. She knew what she wanted. "Oh please, I would like to play with some children outside of the castle's walls."

"Not a problem," said Whiz. Immediately, she was on a playground in the middle of a dodgeball game. Because she did not know the rules, she was hit by the ball and out of the game. That was not fun. The next game was tag, but she did not know that she was supposed to run, so she was always caught. She was, therefore, always "it." She was exhausted. She was not sure that playing with other children was fun. She wanted to go home but did not know exactly where it was.

Luckily, the guards who were looking for her came by. When she saw them, she jumped for joy. She jumped so high that she landed on the back of a guard's horse, and she rode home in record time.

Circle the word that describes how Priscilla feels in each situation.

1.	When the guards are watching her:	angry	unhappy	contented
2.	When she is lost in the woods:	frightened	tired	free
3.	When she is granted a wish:	disappointed	elated	scared
4.	When she plays dodgeball and tag:	hurt	playful	discouraged
5.	When she sees the guards:	relieved	resentful	encouraged

A Day at the Lake

Read the passage.

Erika and Abby rode together in the backseat. They were excited because they were going to the lake. Erika had never been to the lake before. She was going with her best friend Abby and Abby's family.

Abby told Erika all about the sand and the waves. She also told her about the paddleboat. "I like to paddle to the deep part of the lake and jump into the water," said Abby. Erika felt her stomach tighten. She did not know how to swim. She did not know that Abby was so brave in the water. Erika did not say anything.

On the shore of the lake, the girls had a great time. They played in the water. They built a huge sand castle using buckets and shovels. Then, they let water in and created a moat. Erika thought that the lake was great!

Abby's dad called for them to come to the boat dock. He had the paddleboat ready for them and held two life jackets in his hands. Abby ran to the boat, put on her life jacket, and sat down. She smiled and waited for Erika. Erika was very nervous. Abby's dad helped her put on her life jacket. Erika carefully climbed into the seat and put her feet on the pedals. Abby started pedaling, so Erika did, too. Soon, they were moving quickly across the water. Erika was having fun. When they were far out on the lake, Abby stopped the boat and said, "Last one in the lake has stinky feet!" Abby jumped into the water. Erika did not move. She did not dare tell Abby that she could not swim. Would Abby laugh at her?

Abby watched Erika. Finally, she said, "Are you coming in?" When Erika shrugged her shoulders, Abby guessed what was wrong. She climbed back into the boat. "Do you know how to swim yet?" she asked kindly. Erika shook her head. Abby smiled at her friend and said, "OK. Let's paddle around some more. After lunch, I'll teach you a little bit about swimming." Erika smiled at her best friend. Why had she ever worried about telling Abby that she did not know how to swim?

A Day at the Lake

Answer the questions using complete sentences.

1. What do you think Abby would have done if Erika told her earlier that she did not know how to swim?

_____

2. Why do you think Erika waits to tell Abby that she cannot swim?

_____

3. How can Abby tell that Erika does not know how to swim?

_____

4. How do you think Erika can learn how to swim?

_____

5. What do the girls have fun doing at the lake?

_____

6. Do you think that Abby will invite Erika to the lake again? Why or why not?

_____

7. Do you think that Erika will go to the lake again if she is invited? Why or why not?

_____

Circle the words that best describe each girl.

8. What is Erika like?

- bossy
- quiet
- cautious
- selfish
- a bad listener
- a worrier
- brave
- nervous
- unafraid
- a bad friend

9. What is Abby like?

- bossy
- helpful
- brave
- caring
- a bad listener
- cautious
- kind
- nervous
- selfish
- a good friend

Helen Keller

Read the passage and answer the questions.

Helen Keller was a well-known woman. She was born in 1880. When she was 19 months old, she suffered from a terrible illness that left her unable to see, hear, and speak. For several years, young Helen lived in complete darkness and silence. She was angry and afraid and acted wildly.

When Helen was seven years old, her teacher, Ann Sullivan, taught her to "hear" and "speak" with her hands. After that, Helen learned quickly. She even learned to use her voice. When she was older, Helen went to college and graduated with honors.

Helen was very smart and dedicated. She wrote books and gave many speeches. She worked hard to teach others about coping with disabilities. She also worked against unfairness and violence against people. Helen Keller became very famous and lived until she was 88 years old.

1. List four of Helen Keller's greatest accomplishments (hard things that she did).

_____

_____

2. Choose one of her accomplishments and write why it was hard for Helen.

_____

3. Write four words that describe Helen Keller.

HELEN KELLER

4. Imagine that you cannot see, hear, and talk. What is different about your day? Tell about one change that you would have to make in your morning, afternoon, and evening routines.

Morning: _____

Afternoon: _____

Evening: _____

Rattlesnakes

There are different reasons for reading. Sometimes, you might read to find specific information or to study for a test. Other times, you might read for personal enjoyment. Depending on the purpose of the reading task, different skills are put to use. **Finding the facts** of a passage means that you can respond to specific questions with precise answers.

Read the story. Then, circle the letters next to facts that complete each sentence.

Rattlesnakes are poisonous reptiles that live anywhere from southern Canada in North America to Argentina in South America. There are 31 species of rattlesnakes. The majority live in the southwestern United States and in Mexico. Most rattlesnakes stay away from open spaces where they are unprotected from predators, and they usually avoid contact with humans. They spend much of their time under rocks, logs, debris, and shrubs.

A rattlesnake has excellent eyesight and a great sense of smell. Its forked tongue senses a combination of smells and tastes. It has ears, but they cannot receive outside sounds, since an external and a middle ear cavity are missing. It has an inner ear that enables it to detect ground vibrations.

The rattlesnake has two long teeth called fangs. The fangs inject a bitten animal with the snake's poison, or venom. Rattlesnakes hunt and eat rodents, small birds, lizards, and frogs. Because snakes digest food slowly, a rattlesnake may not hunt for several days.

The rattlesnake's rattle is probably its best-known feature. It is a series of interlocking segments that vibrate whenever the tail shakes. Rattlesnakes are very dangerous. If you hear a rattlesnake's rattle, do not go near the snake.

1. Rattlesnakes are   **A.** good.   **B.** pets.   **C.** reptiles.   **D.** poisonous.

2. Rattlesnakes have   **A.** fangs.   **B.** rattles.   **C.** colors.   **D.** no ears.

3. Rattlesnakes eat   **A.** rodents.   **B.** small birds.   **C.** grass.   **D.** bugs.

4. Rattlesnakes live   **A.** in Mexico.   **B.** in Alaska.   **C.** under rocks.   **D.** in groups.

5. Rattlesnakes can   **A.** talk.   **B.** see.   **C.** smell.   **D.** hear.

Taking Care of Teeth

Read the passage.

Long ago, people cleaned their teeth in interesting ways. They scratched their teeth with a stick, wiped them with a rag, or even chewed on crushed bones or shells. Tooth care has come a long way in the past few hundred years. Now, we have fluoride toothpaste, dental floss, and specially angled toothbrushes to keep our teeth healthy.

It took someone with a lot of time on his hands to invent the first toothbrush. In the 1770s, a man named William Addis was in prison. While he was wiping his teeth with a rag, he had the idea to make a tool for cleaning teeth. He used a bone and some bristles from a hairbrush. He carefully drilled holes in one end of the bone. Then, he trimmed the brush bristles and pushed them into the holes that he had drilled. He glued the bristles into place and had the first toothbrush.

People have used different tooth cleaners over the years. Many cleaners, such as crushed bones and shells, actually damaged the protective enamel on teeth. Chalk was a popular cleaner in the 1850s. Baking soda was also used for many years, because it was abrasive. Some toothpastes still contain baking soda. Other people used salt as a tooth cleaner. Many of today's toothpastes contain sodium, too. Fluoride was first added to toothpaste in 1956 and greatly reduced the number of cavities in children. Most recently, calcium was added to toothpaste in the 1960s to help strengthen teeth.

Using dental floss once a day is one of the most important things that you can do for your teeth. Originally, the thin string was made of silk. Now, dental floss comes in different colors and flavors, tape, and waxed and unwaxed varieties. Dental floss removes "interproximal plaque accumulation," which means that it scrapes off the plaque between your teeth, where a toothbrush cannot reach.

The inventions and improvements in dental care have helped people maintain stronger, healthier teeth. We now know how to care for our teeth every day.

Taking Care of Teeth

Circle the letter next to the answer.

1. Why did the author write this passage?

    A. to entertain   **B.** to teach   **C.** to sell something

2. What kind of passage is "Taking Care of Teeth"?

    A. a factual passage   **B.** a humorous passage   **C.** a fictional passage

3. What is the main idea of the passage?

    A. how to take care of teeth   **B.** the importance of flossing   **C.** the history of dental care

Complete the diagram with details from the passage (page 76).

The Importance of Dental Floss

_____

_____

_____

Tooth Cleaners Over the Years

_____

_____

_____

Tooth Care

Tooth Cleaning Today

_____

_____

_____

The Invention of the Toothbrush

_____

_____

_____

Wolves

Read the passage.

If you have read fairy tales, you may believe that wolves are vicious, evil, and ruthless creatures that hurt people, pigs, and other small animals. You may also believe that they are aggressive and will not stop until they get what they want. There really is not anything good to say about wolves. Or, is there? Are wolves misunderstood?

Wolves are actually nothing like their characters portrayed in fairy tales. It is true that their diet consists of deer, rabbits, and other small animals, but wolves rarely attack people. Wolves have been known to attack people, but only when people threaten them. Wolves are usually shy animals. They stay within their own territories and protect their own packs.

Wolves eat meat, and they must hunt to get their food. They are strong and fast and have sharp teeth. They have a keen sense of smell, hunt in packs, and chase their prey until it gets tired. They usually hunt the weakest, slowest animal in a group. Wolves are not cruel; they are just good hunters.

Some wolves, such as red wolves, are near extinction. They have been hunted extensively, and their homes are steadily disappearing as people spread their own homes further into the wilderness.

Ranchers and farmers pose another threat to wolves. They become angry when wolves come onto their property and eat their livestock. This is a serious problem, because the farmers lose their animals and then begin to hunt the wolves. No one wins in this battle.

Wolves are an important part of the balance of nature. They help keep down the populations of some animals, such as deer. In many countries, it is now against the law to hunt wolves. Many scientists are working hard to protect wolves, because they understand just how important and misunderstood wolves really are.

Wolves

Use the chart to compare the positive and negative characteristics of wolves.

Positive Characteristics	Negative Characteristics

1. Choose one of the negative characteristics from your chart. Write an explanation of why wolves need that trait. Explain why it is natural, not cruel.

    _____

    _____

    _____

2. Write a brief version of a popular fairy tale from the wolf's point of view.

    _____

    _____

    _____

    _____

    _____

    _____

    _____

    _____

    _____

    _____

    _____

Summer Bridge Reading RB-904094

Which Book Have You Read?

Review the diagram. Then, answer the questions.

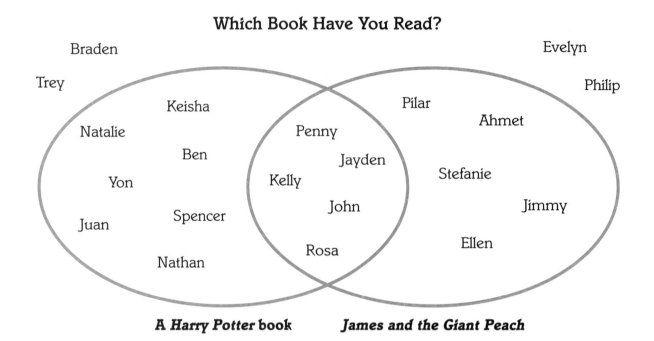

Which Book Have You Read?

Braden

Evelyn

Trey

Philip

Keisha

Pilar

Natalie

Ahmet

Ben

Penny

Yon

Jayden

Kelly

Stefanie

John

Jimmy

Juan

Spencer

Rosa

Ellen

Nathan

A *Harry Potter* book   ***James and the Giant Peach***

1. How many children have read a *Harry Potter* book? _____

2. How many children have not read a *Harry Potter* book?_____

3. How many children were questioned?_____

4. Which children have not read either book? _____

5. How many children have read *James and the Giant Peach*? _____

6. Which children have read both books? _____

Extra! What is your favorite book? What do you think is the best part about that book?

_____

_____

_____

_____

Chewing Gum

Read the passage.

My name is Thomas Adams. You probably have no idea who I am. I invented chewing gum. Actually, *invented* might be a strong word.

I lived in the 1800s. I once met General Santa Anna. He was a military general from Mexico. Santa Anna told me about a dried sap called chicle. He liked to chew this sap, which comes from the sapodilla tree. He said that Mayans and others had been chewing it for hundreds of years. I tried some. Honestly, I thought it tasted terrible.

Still, I was interested in chicle because it was so rubbery. I thought that maybe I could make things, like toys or boots, out of it. But, nothing I tried seemed to work. It would just not replace rubber.

One day, I popped a terrible-tasting piece of chicle in my mouth and chewed and chewed. "Yuck," I thought. "Wouldn't it be nice if it had some flavor?" Eureka! I had a great idea! So, I opened a flavored-gum factory and sold chewing gum like crazy.

Americans loved my gum. But, doctors seemed to think that it was bad. They said that it was bad for people's teeth. That may be true, but one doctor even said, "Chewing gum will exhaust the salivary glands and cause the intestines to stick together." Is that not the silliest thing that you have ever heard?

I am proud to say that flavored chewing gum was a hit, even though no one knows my name!

Chewing Gum

Circle the best answers.

1. How does the author feel about chicle?

    A. friendly   **B.** curious   **C.** disgusted   **D.** angry

2. How does the author feel about flavored chewing gum?

    A. embarrassed   **B.** worried   **C.** proud   **D.** curious

3. What did the author think that the chicle could do?

    A. replace gum   **B.** become rubber   **C.** replace rubber   **D.** ruin teeth

4. What did the author think about what one doctor said?

    A. He was right.   **B.** He was silly.   **C.** He was late.   **D.** He was smart.

Answer the questions using complete sentences.

5. Why does the author think that people should know his name?

_____

_____

6. Write a brief summary of the passage from your own point of view.

_____

_____

_____

7. Write a brief summary of the passage from the point of view of the doctor who did not think that gum was safe.

_____

_____

_____

Paul Bunyan

To **exaggerate** means to make people, things, or events sound bigger or more important than they really are.

Read the passage.

Paul Bunyan was a large boy who was born in the woods of a small town in Maine. Although Paul grew to be very big and strong, he remained a peaceful and kind person. Paul's family business was logging. His father cut down trees and sold them to lumber companies.

Paul was so strong that he could cut down five trees with just one swing of his ax. His father soon grew rich from all of the trees that Paul cut down. The family sold their home in the small town and bought a large area of wilderness in the backwoods of Maine.

In the forest, Paul became friends with wild animals. He wrestled with bears and ran with deer. One day, Paul walked in a snowstorm that left four feet of blue snow on the ground. He stumbled over a cold, shivering, blue ox calf. Paul hugged the animal, warmed him up, and took him home. Paul named the ox Babe. They were friends for life.

When Paul was old enough to leave home, he packed a bag and set off with Babe to see the West. Paul cleared trees as he went and made a path for the pioneers to follow.

Paul's first big job on his trip was to dig a shipping channel so that he could send the logs that he cut to Maine on boats. He spent one day digging out the Great Lakes and the St. Lawrence Seaway. Then, he hired a crew of men to help him clear the Great Plains of trees. After that big job, Paul Bunyan was tired. Letting his ax drag behind him, he carved out the Grand Canyon.

Paul Bunyan and Babe made it to the West Coast and then traveled around the United States some more. Stories say that Paul still lives in the wilderness, where he cares for the animals and trees that need his help.

Paul Bunyan

Answer the questions using complete sentences.

1. Paul Bunyan was a large man, but stories exaggerate his size and strength. Write down five exaggerations from the passage (page 83).

    _____

    _____

    _____

    _____

    _____

2. Write two exaggerations of your own for Paul Bunyan. Make sure that your exaggerations fit where and when he lived.

    Size:_____

    Strength: _____

3. Write an exaggeration about something that you did or about one of your personal characteristics.

    _____

    _____

    _____

    _____

    _____

    _____

    _____

    _____

Alphabetical Order

> Most reference work requires the skill of **alphabetizing**. Dictionaries, encyclopedias, and other reference materials are organized alphabetically.
>
> Sometimes, it is necessary to look at only the first letter when you are alphabetizing a list.
> **Example:** alligator   crocodile   iguana   turtle
>
> Other times, you must look at the second, third, or fourth letters of words when the first letter of each word is the same.
> **Example:** raspberries   reasonable   roast   runt

Number each list alphabetically.

1. _____ capital
_____ creek
_____ ceiling
_____ chime

2. _____ shrink
_____ shirt
_____ sheet
_____ shut

3. _____ elevate
_____ eventually
_____ elementary
_____ evaporate

4. _____ cranium
_____ crawl
_____ crater
_____ crash

5. _____ planet
_____ placement
_____ plural
_____ pleasant

6. _____ aluminum
_____ alignment
_____ allotment
_____ alligator

7. _____ finisher
_____ freedom
_____ finger
_____ furniture

8. _____ scholarship
_____ schnauzer
_____ schooner
_____ scheme

9. _____ whether
_____ white
_____ whistle
_____ wheat

What Do You Want to Know?

When you are looking up information in reference materials, such as an encyclopedia or almanac, ask yourself the question, what am I trying to find? Answer the question and notice the **key words**. The key words tell you what to look up.

Examples: Where was William <u>Shakespeare</u> born? (Usually, look up a person by his last name.)

Who was <u>Napoleon</u>? (Some people are best known by their first names.)

Who surrendered to General Ulysses <u>Grant</u> to end the <u>Civil War</u>? (Sometimes, more than one reference or key word is given.)

Read each possible reference question and underline the key words.

1. Where is Venetian glass made?

2. Who was the 32nd United States President?

3. Why is there concern about wolves becoming extinct?

4. What were gladiators, and when were they prominent?

5. Which breeds of dogs are good bird hunters?

6. What was the Treaty of Versailles, and who signed it?

7. Who were the Mayans, and what happened to them?

8. How long does it take Earth to travel around the sun?

9. During what years was the American Revolutionary War fought?

10. What is the longest river in Asia?

11. In what habitat do flamingos live?

12. Where are the migration flyways in Canada?

13. Who were the first settlers in St. Augustine, Florida?

14. In what ways can rattlesnakes be helpful and harmful?

15. How long ago was the Iron Age, and where did people live then?

16. How many nations belong to the United Nations?

17. How long did it take for the Eiffel Tower to be built?

Summer Bridge Reading RB-904094

Book Directories

The **table of contents** and the **index** of a book are directories. The table of contents is in the front of a book. It lists each chapter by its title or subject. If a book has an index, it is at the end. The index lists specific names and subjects in alphabetical order, as well as the precise page or pages where information about them can be found.

Using the table of contents and the index, write the page numbers on which you would look to answer the questions. Write *NG* if the page number is not given.

Table of Contents

Index

	Table of Contents	Index
1. Why is Mars called "the red planet"?	_____	_____
2. Who invented the telescope?	_____	_____
3. How are the stars grouped to form Ursa Major?	_____	_____
4. What is the temperature of the sun?	_____	_____
5. What is the difference between a meteor and a meteorite?	_____	_____
6. Which planet is the largest?	_____	_____

A Specialized Dictionary

> A **glossary** is a specialized dictionary. It is usually at the back of a specialized reference book and has words that pertain to only the subjects covered in the book.

Several words are listed in order as they would be in a glossary. Decide what the subject of the book is. Then, circle the letter next to the title of the book.

1. cardinal, finch, nuthatch, oriole

   A. *Birds of the Backyard*   **B.** *Birds of Prey*   **C.** *Waterbirds*

2. Little Dipper, Milky Way, North Star, Orion

   A. *Navigator at Night*   **B.** *Darkness*   **C.** *Night Sky*

3. canoe, kayak, skiff

   A. *Kinds of Fish*   **B.** *Small Recreational Boats*   **C.** *Fishing Boats*

4. hounds, retrievers, springer spaniels, terriers

   A. *Choosing a Pet*   **B.** *Breeds of Dogs*   **C.** *Training Your Dog*

5. air pressure, cold front, humidity, precipitation

   A. *Dog Days of Summer*   **B.** *Four Seasons*   **C.** *Weather Forecasting*

6. leopard, ocelot, panther, puma

   A. *Wild Pets*   **B.** *Big Cats*   **C.** *Circus Animals*

7. London, New York, Paris, Tokyo

   A. *World Cities*   **B.** *World Countries*   **C.** *World Connections*

8. Chinese, French, German, Spanish

   A. *Countries*   **B.** *United Nations*   **C.** *Languages*

9. Africa, Australia, Europe, South America

   A. *People of Other Countries*   **B.** *Continents*   **C.** *World Countries*

10. Ford's Theatre, Lincoln Memorial, Pentagon, the U.S. Capitol

   A. *Washington, D.C.*   **B.** *The U.S. Government*   **C.** *U.S. Presidents*

Guide Words

Use **guide words** to help you find a word in a dictionary. Guide words are the two words at the top of each dictionary page. Any entry word listed on that page will fall alphabetically between the guide words.

Examples: choice—chop   grand—grape   peddle—peg
                        choose   granola   peep

Listed below are sets of guide words. Circle the entry words below each guide word that would be found on that page.

1. badger—bird	**2.** ink—javelin	**3.** penguin—play
bald	impossible	platypus
black	item	peach
baby	jamboree	please
beach	jaw	peace
bicycle	irate	photograph
braid	inch	pepper
4. riot—rustic	**5.** masquerade—mill	**6.** send—sharp
risky	mask	simple
romp	matter	shaft
rumor	money	settle
reaper	mice	shave
rouse	mosque	select
reason	mile	sleek
7. thermos—time	**8.** angora—archery	**9.** comma—cone
thrash	angle	concert
tickle	answer	compare
thank	arena	comfort
threat	anyone	condition
timid	apology	confront
timber	arcade	combat

Summer Bridge Reading RB-904094

So Much Information

An **encyclopedia** is a book, or set of books, containing information on various subjects. The subjects are organized alphabetically. On the outside of each book, a letter or letters show alphabetically what subjects will be found inside the book. Encyclopedias also have guide words at the top of each page to help you locate the subject.

Underline the key word or words that you would use to find the answer to each of the following questions. On the line, write the number of the volume in which the answer can be found.

1. _____ In what civilizations were mummies a part of the burial routine?

2. _____ What countries use the euro for money?

3. _____ What are good uses of nuclear energy?

4. _____ For what is John Philip Sousa best remembered?

5. _____ What is the social life of a honeybee?

6. _____ To whom is the Caldecott Medal awarded?

7. _____ Where was the first tennis match played?

8. _____ What countries have capitalist economies?

9. _____ What are the differences in the number of teeth of a six-year-old child, a twelve-year-old child, and an adult?

10. _____ Why are longitude lines used?

11. _____ What kind of a holiday is Yom Kippur, and who observes it?

12. _____ What is the natural habitat of the raccoon?

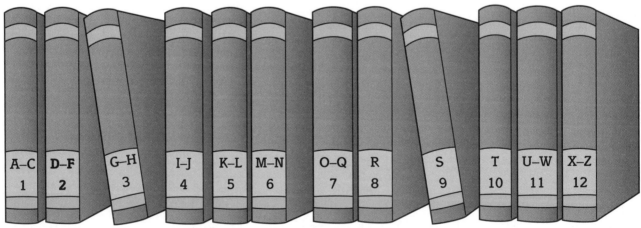

Illinois

An **atlas** is a reference book of maps. The maps may be of states, countries, or the world. Sometimes, an atlas includes informative tables or other factual matter. Some atlases are specialized and might include maps of the night sky, rivers, or populations.

Use the map of Illinois to answer the questions.

1. What major river runs along the western side of Illinois?

   _____

2. About how many miles is it from Quincy to Danville?

   _____

3. What is the state's capital?

   _____

4. How many states border Illinois? _____

5. Which direction do you have to travel to go from East St. Louis to Chicago? _____

6. What is the most southern city in Illinois? _____

7. What bodies of water, besides the Mississippi River, help define Illinois' borders?

   _____

8. If you live in Rantoul, which bordering state would be the closest to you? _____

Summer Bridge Reading RB-904094

Plan It Out

outlining

A good way to organize a story or an article is to make an **outline** of it. Example 1 shows how any paragraph can be outlined. Example 2 shows an actual paragraph and how it could be outlined. Use short phrases for each idea.

Example 1:   I.   Main Idea
A. First supporting idea
B. Second supporting idea

Example 2:   The killdeer has a funny way of distracting its enemies. When it feels it or its nest is in danger, it will pretend to be injured by stumbling along the ground and dragging one of its wing. When it feels that the danger is gone, the killdeer will fly off.

I.   The killdeer distracts enemies.
A. pretends to be injured
B. flies off when the danger is gone

Below are three mixed up outlines. Rewrite them in the correct order.

1. Messages sent over telegraph

Morse code invented

Named after inventor

I. _____

A. _____

B. _____

2. Questions asked

Events discussed

Meeting called to order

I. _____

A. _____

B. _____

3. Nebraska in central United States

Covered by plains

Surrounded by five states

I. _____

A. _____

B. _____

Answer Key

Page 9

1. trip; 2. plans; 3. required;
4. sprinkling; 5. pupils; 6. country;
7. welcomed; 8. constructed;
9. finished; 10. place

Page 10

1. downplay, exaggerate; 2. allow,
refuse; 3. lose, find; 4. stormy,
calm; 5. answer, question; 6. tiny,
enormous; 7. tardy, prompt;
8. relaxed, tense; 9. trash, treasure;
10. reduce, increase; Answers will
vary.

Page 11

1. bough, Answers will vary.;
2. bored, Answers will vary.;
3. herd, Answers will vary.;
4. through, Answers will vary.;
5. ark, Answers will vary.; 6. which,
Answers will vary.; 7. way, Answers
will vary.; 8. grate, Answers will vary.

Page 12

2. pre/determine, to know or decide
before it happens; 3. re/draw, to
draw again; 4. mis/interpret, to
misunderstand or be mistaken; 5.
non/violent, peaceful; 6. dis/agree, to
oppose or contradict; 7. in/take, to
consume/take within; 8. pre/pay, to
pay in advance; 9. un/tie, opposite of
"to tie"; 10. re/name, to name again

Page 13

1. verb, entertainment, noun;
2. noun, peaceful, adjective or
adverb; 3. adverb, verb, preposition,
adjective, or noun, outward,
adjective, adverb, or noun;
4. verb or noun, thoughtless,
adjective; 5. noun, artist,

Page 13 (continued)

noun; 6. verb, excitable; adjective;
7. noun, relationship, noun; 8. noun,
musical, adjective or noun

Page 14

1. C.; 2. C.; 3. B.; 4. B.; 5. A.; 6. C.;
7. B.; 8. B.

Page 15

1. E., N.; 2. B., H.; 3. A., L., R.; 4. D.,
P., T.; 5. F., V.; 6. C., O.; 7. K., M.;
8. I., U., W.; 9. G., Q.; 10. J., S.

Page 16

1. Astronomy; 2. especially;
3. telescope; 4. conditions;
5. observations; 6. constellations;
7. expedition

Page 17

1. park; 2. pet; 3. rock; 4. crack;
5. stick; 6. watch

Page 18

1. midnight; 2. mouse; 3. shiny;
4. flat; 5. swings; 6. howled like a
banshee; 7. excited as bees in a
bonnet; 8. flew like a rocket;
9. looked like a stuffed pig;
10. mad as a wet hen; 11. loud as
100 marching bands

Page 19

1. circled words: row and soldiers,
comparison: the way they stand;
2. circled words: cars and ants,
comparison: cars looked as small
as ants; 3. circled words: clowns
and sardines, comparison: tightly
packed; 4. circled words: lapping
and slopping, comparison: sound
the same; 5. circled words: feet
and drums, comparison: rhythmic
pounding

Page 20

1. C.; 2. A.; 3. B.; 4. A.; 5. B.; 6. A.;
7. B.; 8. A.; 9. B.; 10. C.

Page 21

1. addition; 2. car; 3. tropics;
4. train; 5. trout; 6. canyon;
7. fingers; 8. safe; 9. blue; 10. store;
11. keys; 12. squirrel; 13. cows;
14. stand; 15. tornado

Page 22

1. letter; 2. strong; 3. trail; 4. cow;
5. swift; 6. cradle; 7. wood;
8. sparrow; 9. brother; 10. corn

Page 23

1. The alarm did not go off in the
Cole house, and everyone overslept.
Charlie had to run to catch the school
bus. When Charlie found a seat and
sat down, he ate the apple that he
had grabbed on his way out the door.
If he had eaten breakfast at home, he
would have had a three-mile walk to
school.; 2. Charlie was glad to be on
the bus, because today was a special
day at school. It was Field Day. That
meant the entire school was divided
into teams: red, white, blue, green,
yellow, and orange. Charlie was
wearing a green shirt because he was
on the green team.

Page 24

3, 1, 5, 2, 6, 7, 4, 9, 8;
2, 6, 5, 3, 1, 4

Page 26

1. 5, 1, 10, 4, 9, 7, 2, 8, 3, 11, 6, 12;
2.–3. Answers will vary.

Answer Key

Page 27

Page 28

A. difficult; B. air pressure;
C. Answers and pictures will vary.

Page 30

1. Antonio; 2. to find a place for the lizards so that he doesn't hurt them;
3. He puts them in an aquarium.;
4. his father; 5. Los Angeles;
6. winter; 7. February; Stories will vary.

Page 32

1. Rob, mom, dad, neighbors, neighbors' kids, and fifth-grade friends; 2. Rob; 3. Answers will vary.; 4. Rob needs money to go on a school trip.; 5. to earn half of the money and receive the other half from his parents; 6. He babysits, helps neighbors with yard work, and delivers newspapers.; 7. yes;
8. great, happy; 9. Answers will vary.

Page 33

1. who; 2. what; 3. where; 4. why;
5. when; Stories will vary.

Page 34

One reason to classify animals is to determine which ones are related to each other.; Monkey and apes belong to a group called primates.; Early primates probably ate insects, but they probably also ate leaves and fruits.

Page 35

1. B.; 2. A.; 3. B.; Answers will vary.

Page 36

1. B.; 2. B.; 3. C.

Page 37

Insects are truly amazing animals.; Insects do many of the same things that we do, but they do them in unique ways.; Some insects are beneficial to humans.; Some insects are harmful to humans.; Although all insects have six legs, three body parts, and two antennae, each species of insects is unique.

Page 38

1. B.; 2. A.; 3. C.

Page 39

1. two rungs; 2. when Mike was about two years old; 3. 3;
4. independent; 5. good-sized, ruler, independent; 6. two weeks;
7. reading on patio; 8. animal shelter

Page 40

1. listen, look left, right, left;
2. between parked cars, run, walk slowly, during yellow light; 3. on crosswalk or at corner; 4. carry a flashlight and wear bright clothing;
5. on the left side facing traffic

Page 42

Drawings will vary, but should represent the correct stage of the Saguaro Cactus's life cycle. Labels (clockwise from the top): Seed sprouts, 50 years, animal homes, flowers, fruit, 100 years

Page 44

1. C., some things can be recycled, some things can be composted,

Page 44 (continued)

a compost pile is a pile of leaves, grass, and some kinds of leftover foods that is kept outside.; 2. A., use a small corner of the yard, get a wood box or a bin, put in shredded newspaper, grass, leaves, eggshells, etc.; 3. C., have to stir the pile, needs sunshine, needs water; 4. B., less garbage to throw away, makes good natural fertilizer, is a fun science experiment

Page 45

1. different; 2. different; 3. same;
4. same; 5. different; 6. different

Page 47

1. First-class passengers ate expensive food, had a menu and ate off of china and crystal. Second-class passengers had four-course meals and ate at tables with pretty plates.;
2. There were sitting rooms in first class; 3. In third class, families had cabins and others slept in large rooms with other people. In first and second class, everyone had nice cabins.; 4. They knew that it was special; 1, 2, 1, 3, 2, 3

Page 49

The order of answers will vary.
Blue whale: baleen whale, largest whale, strain food, eat krill and live off blubber in winter, spend summers near North and South Poles, hunted for baleen; *Sperm whale*: toothed whale, largest brain of any animal, stay away from North and South poles, hunted for spermaceti, eat fish, squid, and

Answer Key

Page 49 (continued)

other sea animals; *Both*: mammals, breathe through blowholes, smooth skin, layer of blubber under skin, hunted for meat and blubber

Page 50

1. G.; 2. I.; 3. K.; 4. D.; 5. B.; 6. F.; 7. J.; 8. M.; 9. N.; 10. C.; 11. E.; 12. L.; 13. O.; 14. A.; 15. H.

Page 51

1. cause, effect; 2. effect, cause; 3. effect, cause; 4. cause, effect; 5. effect, cause; 6. effect, cause; 7. cause, effect; 8. effect, cause

Page 52

1. effect; 2. cause; 3. effect; 4. cause; 5. cause; 6. effect; 7. cause; 8. effect

Page 54

1. People move into the house.; 2. People move into the house where the fort is.; 3. The kids cannot play in the fort.; 4. They want to ask if they can play in the fort.; 5. Mrs. Johnson says yes.; 6. They have to play quietly and safely.; 7. The little Johnson kids come to play in the fort.; 8.–9. Answers will vary.

Page 55

1. Fact; 2. Fact; 3. Fact; 4. Fact; 5. Opinion; 6. Opinion; 7. Fact; 8. Fact; 9. Opinion; 10. Fact; 11. Opinion; 12. Fact

Page 56

1. Fact; 2. Opinion; 3. Fact; 4. Opinion; 5. Fact; 6. Opinion; 7. Fact; 8. Fact; 9. Opinion; 10. Fact

Page 57

1.–3. Answers will vary.

Page 58

Answers will vary.

Page 60

1. Chris hears his uncle ask, "Are you all right?"; 2. Chris pushes the covers back.; 3. Chris's uncle says that he went out to the shed to check on the rabbits.; 4. Chris's uncle has a flashlight.; 5. Chris's uncle takes him out to see the rabbits.; 6. Chris puts on his pajamas and goes to sleep.; Stories will vary.

Page 62

1.–2. Answers will vary.; 3. no; 4. yes; 5. on a mountain trail; 6. summer; 7. Yes, the "parents always say the hike is the destination itself," and "I knew better than to ask how much farther we had to go"; 8. Sight, sound, and smell, Answers will vary.; B., F., G., H.

Page 63

Friday Only: Two Pounds for the Price of One.

Page 64

1. B.; 2. A.; 3. C.; 4. C.; 5. A.; 6. C.; Answers will vary.

Page 66

1. They take the shortcut home.; 2. They stay calm and then jump off the tracks.; 3. They take the shortcut in the first place, especially with smaller kids.; 4. Answers will vary.; 5. They were scared.; 6. The narrator says so in the story.

Page 68

1. They should be brave and have a lot of training ; 2. It should be left when it is a natural fire from lightning

Page 68 (continued)

and there is no threat to buildings, etc.; 3. It is a fire that firefighters set to control overgrowth.; 4. It would burn up the oxygen and forest debris of the larger fire so that it has nothing to burn.; 5. It means to put yourself in danger to help others, even if you are scared.; 6. They make sure that it does not get out of control or threaten lives, buildings, etc.; 7. It burns up the overgrowth to allow new trees to grow.; 8. It means to do something without thinking about the consequences.

Page 69

1. A.; 2. D.; 3. C.; 4. B.; 5. B.; 6. C.

Page 70

1. Answers will vary.; 2. husband, Answers will vary.; 3. Answers will vary.

Page 71

1. unhappy; 2. frightened; 3. elated; 4. discouraged; 5. relieved;

Page 73

1.–2. Answers will vary.; 3. Erika did not want to jump into the water.; 4. Answers will vary.; 5. They have fun building sand castles, playing in the water, and pedaling in the paddleboat.; 6.–7. Answers will vary.; 8. quiet, cautious, a worrier, nervous; 9. helpful, brave, caring, kind, a good friend

Page 74

1. learned sign language, graduated from college, wrote books, gave speeches, taught others; 2.–4. Answers will vary.

Answer Key

Page 75
1. C., D.; 2. A., B.; 3. A., B.; 4. A., C.;
5. B., C.

Page 77
1. B.; 2. A.; 3. C.; The importance
of dental floss: to get between
teeth where toothbrush cannot
reach; Tooth cleaners over the
years: crushed bones and shells,
salt, baking soda, chalk; Tooth
cleaning today: toothbrushes,
toothpaste, floss; The invention of
the toothbrush: William Addis, bone
and bristles

Page 79
Answers will vary.; 1.–2. Answers
will vary.

Page 80
1. 12; 2. 9; 3. 21; 4. Trey, Braden,
Evelyn, Philip; 5. 10; 6. Penny, Kelly,
Jayden, John, Rosa; Answers will
vary.

Page 82
1. B., C.; 2. C.; 3. C.; 4. B.; 5. gum
became popular.; 6.–7. Answers will
vary.

Page 84
1. He cut down five trees with one
swing, dug out the Great Lakes and
St. Lawrence Seaway in one day,
cleared the Great Plains of trees, ran
with deer, wrestled with bears, made
a path for pioneers, and carved the
Grand Canyon.; 2.–3. Answers will
vary.

Page 85
1. 1, 4, 2, 3; 2. 3, 2, 1, 4; 3. 2, 4, 1,
3; 4. 1, 4, 3, 2; 5. 2, 1, 4, 3; 6. 4, 1,
3, 2; 7. 2, 3, 1, 4; 8. 3, 2, 4, 1;
9. 2, 4, 3, 1

Page 86
1. Venetian glass; 2. 32nd United
States President; 3. wolves, extinct;
4. gladiators; 5. dogs, bird hunters;
6. Treaty of Versailles; 7. Mayans;
8. Earth, sun; 9. American
Revolutionary War; 10. longest river,
Asia; 11. flamingos; 12. migration
flyways, Canada; 13. settlers,
St. Augustine, Florida;
14. rattlesnakes; 15. Iron Age;
16. United Nations; 17. Eiffel Tower

Page 87
1. TOC: 13; Index: 17–18; 2. TOC:
5; Index: NG; 3. TOC: 33; Index:
35–36; 4. TOC: 27; Index: NG;
5. TOC: 45; Index: NG; 6. TOC: 13;
Index: NG

Page 88
1. A.; 2. C.; 3. B.; 4. B.; 5. C.; 6. B.;
7. A.; 8. C.; 9. B.; 10. A.

Page 89
1. bald, beach, bicycle; 2. item,
jamboree, irate; 3. platypus,
photograph, paper; 4. risky, romp,
rumor, rouse; 5. matter, mice,
mile; 6. shaft, settle; 7. thrash,
tickle, threat, timber; 8. answer,
anyone, apology, arcade; 9. concert,
compare, condition

Page 90
1. mummies, 6; 2. euro, 2;
3. nuclear energy, 6; 4. Sousa, 9;
5. honeybee, 3; 6. Caldecott Medal, 1;
7. tennis, 10; 8. capitalist, 1; 9. teeth,
10; 10. longitude lines, 5; 11. Yom
Kippur, 12; 12. raccoon, 8

Page 91
1. Mississippi; 2. 200; 3. Springfield;
4. 5; 5. Northeast; 6. Cairo; 7. Ohio
River, Wabash River, Lake Michigan;
8. Indiana

Page 92
1. I. Morse code invented; A. Named
after inventor; B. Messages sent over
telegraph; 2. I. Meeting called to
order; A. Events discussed;
B. Questions asked; 3. I. Nebraska in
Central United States; A. Surrounded
by five states; B. Covered by plains

Summer Bridge Reading RB-904094